Christianity and Communism

TODAY

John C. Bennett

ASSOCIATION PRESS
NEW YORK

CHRISTIANITY AND COMMUNISM TODAY

———

———

Association Press, 291 Broadway, New York, N. Y.   10007

Fifth Printing, 1970

Standard Book Number
Hardbound edition: 8096-1779-X
Paperback edition: 8096-1761-7

Library of Congress Catalog Card Number: 60-6553

Printed in the United States of America

Preface

THIS BOOK was first published in 1948 during the early days of the cold war. I am willing to have it reprinted in 1970 only because I believe that its basic outlook remains valid even as my own thought about the subject has developed to the position summarized in the new Introduction. In 1948 I avoided the crusading type of opposition to Communism and emphasized that Communism was a judgment upon Christians and churches. I wrote originally when Stalinism was the dominant Communist force in the world and much of my criticism of Communism was directed against Stalinism. Mao's Communism had not yet established control in China and the present interest in Asian Communism in general was not much in our minds.

In the new edition in 1960 I added an introduction about the changes in Communist nations since 1948. This is now replaced by a new Introduction for 1970. Also, in 1960, I added three chapters which remain in this edition as Chapters 3, 7 and 8. A few editorial changes were made to update the book at that time. The chapters on the nature of Communism as a total system and on the issues that separate it from Christianity remain as I wrote them in 1948 because they have stood up well under criticism since that time. I think that they are still essentially correct when we are thinking of Communism as

3

such a total system. My present attitude toward the subject—which is essentially the same as my attitude in 1960 —is based on the fact that we have no longer to deal with Communism as an international, monolithic system of life and thought, but with particular kinds of Communism as they have developed in individual nations or persons.

I can now quote President Nixon's report on foreign policy sent to the Congress of February 18, 1970 to support this perspective. He said the following about Communism:

> Then, (during the post-war period) we were confronted by a monolithic Communist world. Today, the nature of that world has changed—the power of individual Communist nations has grown, but international Communist unity has been shattered. Once a unified bloc, its solidarity has been broken by the powerful forces of nationalism.

This represents a change in the President's own characteristic attitude toward Communism and, obvious as the facts underlying that statement were, its truth was never fully assimilated by the policy-makers under Lyndon Johnson. The Vietnam policy has been based in part on the old assumption of a unified international Communist threat that should be stopped within Vietnam, at whatever cost to Vietnamese or Americans, rather than at some later time at a point closer to us.

If I were writing Chapter 7 today I should use American policy in Vietnam as a striking example of what not to do. Years of war have shown the limits of American power in solving the internal political problems of Vietnam. They also show that anti-Communism as a motive and a policy can turn Americans into agents of technological destruction on a scale that is vast and terrible. I hope that we have learned from this experience and that we will not use our military power again to try to prevent other nations from having revolutions even when there is a strong Communist factor in those revolutions.

Chapter 8 says things that needed to be said in 1960 but today I should have less patience with those who raise questions about the morality of co-existence. As I write these words the American government in many ways is affirming a policy that looks beyond co-existence to the beginnings of a more positive relationship with Communist China and to cooperation in the interests of world security with the Soviet Union. Though there are still moralists and religious people who argue against co-existence and there are still anti-Communist crusaders, they do not determine policy and they have little influence on the national trends of public opinion. One significant straw in the wind was the change in the editorial policy of *Time* magazine. It has been one of the chief supporters of the conventional forms of anti-Communism, especially in its opposition to a more open policy in relation to mainland China, but on June 6, 1969 it carried an editorial calling for a new China policy, for steps leading to a possible rapprochement between the United States and Communist China. It is a cautious statement but the steps it advocates are in the opposite direction from that long associated with *Time*.

Chapter 9 was the final chapter of the 1948 edition. I allow it to stand because it does summarize what the original edition tried to say and a comparison of it with my new Introduction may quickly indicate the contrast between the stance of the original book and what after twenty-two years I believe we should say about the subject. Readers can judge whether there is continuity in spirit.

JOHN C. BENNETT

Contents

A New Introduction: 1970

It is the purpose of this Introduction to sketch the changes that have come in Communism since 1948 which make it essential for Christians to think differently about their relations with Communist nations or with Communists as people. American Christians need to ask themselves how the United States should deal with particular nations that have Communist regimes and that are quite different from one another, and how they as Christians should discuss religious and political problems with a new breed of Marxists. Yet the parts of this book that were written in 1948 throw light on what has brought these nations and these Marxists individuals to their present condition. They may help us to understand some of the hangups and rigidities that remain among Communists and non-Communists today when they seek to establish new relations with each other. Also in some pre-revolutionary situations we may meet Communism or Marxist-Leninism as a system to which people are committed as an absolute faith and doctrine. In their case my exposition of Communism and my discussion of the illusions which it generates and the cruelties to which it is likely to lead is quite relevant. However it is important to remember that revolution and civil disorders usually are cruel.[1]

---

[1] There is a tendency to remember the atrocities of our opponents and conveniently forget those on our side. For example the massacre of 10,000 Taiwanese—including a large proportion of the island's leaders—in 1947 by the representatives of the Chinese na-

I have left unchanged my description of the tyranny and terror of Stalinism in Chapter 2. Stalinism in the main belongs to the past but it remains as a shadow on the present. Moreover, it should not be forgotten what can happen when an absolute totalitarian system goes unchecked. I wrote about it as I saw it then and I do not believe that what I saw was false. Yet today I could not convey as vividly the sense that I had then of the terrible human cost of developments in the Soviet Union. In Chapter 3 I deal with the later stage of these developments under Khrushchev who in spite of great mistakes at home and such international adventures as the placing of missiles in Cuba, was more of a liberalizing leader than his successors. Much in that chapter remains true but today I have less hope than I had when I wrote it of an early realization of cultural freedom in Russia. There is an oppressive grayness about Soviet society, not the all-pervasive terror of Stalinism but intimidation of all independent spirits. The leadership fears change and seeks to avoid contamination by ideas from abroad, from the humanistic form of Communism in Czechoslovakia which has been largely suppressed by Russian power.

---

tionalists is generally forgotten except by the Taiwanese (A. Doak Barnett: *Communist China and Asia,* Harper, 1960, p. 389). And in 1966 the anti-Communists in Indonesia slaughtered about 400,000 people in a few weeks but, while this was regretted by people on our side, the effects were welcomed and it has never been emphasized as an example of how in times of civil war we can expect atrocities on both sides. The massacre at Song My of Vietnam villagers by American soldiers reveals the degree of brutality to which our own people can descend in a guerrilla war. Yet, we have to ask how much this killing of children and other civilians at short range is different from air strikes against large zones which are known to contain helpless non-combatants. One of the hardest things to live with today is the pervasiveness of political cruelty, of the willingness to kill, torture and imprison political opponents in a great variety of situations.

There is in the Soviet Union considerable intellectual ferment just below the surface. The authorities can no longer count on ideological loyalty, on the prevalence of Communism as a faith among the younger generation. Intellectuals are punished by prison and exile and yet their supporters continue to speak out and their protests frequently become news outside of the Soviet Union.

The invasion of Czechoslovakia brought out much of this protest within Russia and it has caused many in the west to wonder if we are not back where we were in the days of Stalin's terror. Hateful as that Soviet policy is in itself it is being carried on with some inhibitions because of world opinion and because of the strong opposition from many Communist parties. The humanistic Communism in Czechoslovakia that it seeks to destroy was dominant within the Communist party itself. The invasion of Czechoslovakia was a desperate effort to prevent change in Soviet society and it was prompted by genuine fear that Czechoslovakia would militarily become a soft spot in the defense of the Warsaw Pact nations. It was not a first step in a new policy of unlimited aggression whether out of commitment to world revolution or arising from an indefinitely expansionist imperialism. The Russians were afraid of losing what they thought they had.

What I have just said may seem too dogmatic and all of us are forced to calculate without hard facts. The impression of indecisiveness and fear and weakness rather than of ideological confidence and of strong national will in the case of the Soviet leaders governs what I have said. The fear of being involved in conflict with both China and the United States explains much of the Soviet stance. China may not be a military danger but the sheer weight of the Chinese population on its borders in the long run can be a threat.

The Soviet Union and the United States have a history of ideological messianism but I suspect that this is weaker now in the Soviet Union than in the United States though recent lessons have reduced its power in this country. The most important fact about both nations is that they are superpowers with each having the capacity to destroy the other many times over. Each fears the other and the remnants of ideology make communication difficult. The issues that now separate these two powers have very little to do with the contrast between Christianity and Communism.

I can illustrate this by referring to the issues that separate the United States and the Soviet Union in the Middle East. Like the Russia of the Czars, the Soviet Union has long sought to be a Mediterranean power. It has chosen to win Arab friendship, partly for that reason and partly because the Arab nations belong to "the third world" which the Soviet Union seeks to win as its sphere of influence in competition with China. It uses ideology as an instrument but it is doubtful if its real goals are different from those of great powers in other periods. The United States seeks to prevent a marked upset in the balance of power in the Middle East, for the sake of world stability and to keep Israel from being destroyed. Our national interest in the security of Israel does have an ideological element in it, in so far as we feel kinship with Israel as a democratic society in a hostile environment, but there is also a human concern to prevent another Jewish holocaust. Also any American government will be responsive to the fact that so many of its citizens (not only Jews) have a very close tie with Israel. The American government will want to avoid being put into the position either of having to intervene militarily or of having to allow Israel to be destroyed. Israel can at present more than protect herself, but some years from now Soviet support of Arab nations could change the situation and confront the United States with a most difficult choice involving the possibility of world war. All of this could go on even if there were no Communists or Christians involved. The conflicting claims of Arabs and Israelis which are at the heart of the problem and which represent such a tragic stalemate belong to a different world of discourse than the discussions of the issues dividing Christians from Communists.

The most important change that affects the meaning of Communism today is the fact that the Communist world is now broken into pieces. As is often said, the Communist "monolith" no longer exists and the spectre of it should no longer control American national policy or our personal attitudes. This process began with the development of a national Communism in Yugoslavia. In 1949 the Communist Party of Yugoslavia renounced its ties with the Party in the Soviet Union and Tito's nation began to adopt an independent policy at home and in its relation with other nations. Ever since then it has tried to maintain a neutralist foreign policy and it has encouraged relations with the West. At home it has moved away from tight controls on the culture and on individual expression. It still calls itself a Communist country but its economic policies are no longer controlled by a rigid ideology and as a community its windows and doors are open to the world. It demonstrated twenty years ago that Communism need not have only one meaning and this was the beginning of what now is the pluralistic nature of Communism.

The split between the Soviet Union and China was the most dramatic change of this sort. It was another expression of nationalism. There has been a long history of conflict between Russia and China as Asian powers separated by a long common boundary. This nationalism has been combined with differences of ideology that lead to mutual accusations of heresy and it is influenced by the fact that the two nations are at different stages in the development of Communism. Even race is a factor. The Soviet Union now must be counted among the relatively wealthy white nations, whereas China is not only non-white but also it seeks still to be the leader of the world's poor. It is much more the revolutionary force, though the Soviet Union and China are rivals for leadership among Communist nations. The involvement of both in Vietnam is more a sign of this rivalry today than it is an example of cooperation between them. Today some observers speak of the possibility and sometimes of the probability of war between these two giants.

This split between the Soviet Union and China has already had an enormous effect on the attitudes of non-Communist Western nations to international Communism. In the 1950's it did appear that the Western nations comprising most of what was called the "free world" were threatened at the same time from East and West, by a vast international power representing the unity of the Soviet Union and China. It is not strange that people in the United States became fearful that the "free world" would become more and more constricted, with its existence threatened by each advance of this worldwide Communist force. As has been stated in the Preface, the official American policy in Vietnam was largely controlled by this view of the world. Today we see that the two great Communist powers fear each other, though both still fear American nuclear power. This is a new situation which opens up possibilities that did not exist when the 1960 edition of this book was published. We can take no comfort from the possibility of armed conflict between the Soviet Union and China. That would be an appalling human disaster in itself and it could become a world war.

The United States confronts a dilemma. How shall we move ahead with a new China policy which now seems acceptable to most of the American people without appearing to become more anti-Soviet at a time when rapprochement with the Soviet Union especially on matters of disarmament is so important for the world's peace and security? The changes that have come in Soviet society since Stalin's time would have more hope in them if Soviet fears could be reduced and if relations between the Soviet people and other peoples could be multiplied.

Diversity among Communist nations is characteristic of the eastern European nations that are in the Soviet sphere of influence. The situation has changed so far as particular nations are concerned since 1960. At that time Poland seemed the Eastern nation with the greatest cultural freedom. Now the Communist government in Poland has become repressive and its fear of Germany accentuates its dependence on the Soviet Union. At that time Czechoslovakia was under a Stalinist regime. I have already referred to the tragic setback in Czechoslovakia after the brief flowering in that country of a form of "Communism with a human face." Rumania, except for Yugoslavia, is the most independent of the eastern countries in its foreign policy and, though its internal institutions show few signs of liberalization, it gave strong moral support to the freedom-loving Czechs. Hungary which lost a revolution in 1956 is now internally one of the freer of these nations. The Kadar regime finally cooperated with the Soviet Union's invasion of Czechoslovakia but is known to have been strongly opposed to it.

East Germany is today under a repressive Stalinist regime though German efficiency has made it the most prosperous of the Eastern nations. For it to remain Communist is especially important for the security of the Russians in relation to the German threat which is so deeply engraved in their memories and there is no early expectation of its greater freedom from Soviet power or of its liberalization. A new German government dominated by the Social Democrats will try to build bridges with East Germany and it remains to be seen if they will have any effect upon the internal life of that country. Détente between East and West, and especially between the United States and West Germany on one side and the Soviet Union on the other, is one essential condition for a continuous movement toward national independence or toward inner liberalization in the Soviet orbit in Europe.

Underlying all of the changes that have come in Communist countries is the fact that, on all sides, the ideological bond within Communist nations and between them has lost most of its power. From one point of view this may be regretted because at its best Communist ideology did have desirable goals. On the other hand it is better for peace and freedom that the aggressive fanaticism of Communism in Europe is dead. A Communist bloc bound together by devotion to Communism as a faith or an ideal or by loyalty to the Soviet Union as the fatherland of Communism no longer is a spectre threatening a long continued spiritual war between East and West that might lead to a military conflict, even to nuclear war. If a military conflict should come, it would be inspired by nationalistic fears and ambitions rather than by Communism as a cause. The Soviet Union is itself more controlled by the desire to prevent a nuclear war than by ideology. This underlies the possibility of diplomatic and military détente between the two great nuclear powers. The nightmare that was common in the West when NATO was established was the possibility of Europe as a whole coming under the military domination of the Soviet Union with a continental Communist movement doing its bidding within each nation. The Soviet Union today does not have the capacity to establish such a center of power for the whole of Europe; it has difficulty enough with its neighbors that once were bound to it by the ideological bond. Nationalism and the human spirit are too strong for the only kind of power that would not be totally self-defeating. It is possible for a nuclear power to create a desert but it would then have no communities over which to rule and no wealth of the conquered to inherit. Moreover the cautious rulers of the Soviet Union do not want to lose face or the appearance of some moral or ideological justification for their policies.

I was impressed by the report of the American Ambassador to Moscow, Mr. Foy D. Kohler, in December 1966. He said:

> Those of you who travel in Europe must be struck by how much less ideological the Europeans have become. The same is true, I can tell you on the basis of my personal experience, of the East Europeans and the Russians. Indeed, precisely because they were exposed to a pernicious and dogmatic ideology, they are in some respects even less ideological than their Western European brothers.
>
> (*U.S. News and World Report,* Dec. 26, 1966)

Richard Rovere, the very perceptive Washington correspondent of *The New Yorker,* goes so far as to say that "Communism is scarcely more binding ideologically than monarchy or democracy." (*The New Yorker,* Feb-

ruary 24, 1968.) What has happened in this regard is
not unexpected if we realize that there has been a change
of generations and a change of functions among the
leaders in these countries. Generations rebel against their
predecessors in East as well as West and in this case a
change of functions has meant that revolutionaries and
conspirators have been necessarily supplanted by builders and planners and technicians, by doctors and edu-
cators. This erosion of ideology may have left an intellectual vacuum in many situations and it may also involve
a movement from a fanatical faith to a dull and rigid
outlook that has difficulty in accepting change or in understanding what is happening in the outside world.
Where these things are true it may be difficult to know
how to communicate with this new generation of Communists, but the old way of engaging in ideological warfare on our part is the most destructive of all ways.

This loss of a consistent ideology as a guide to life and
as the source of a powerful spiritual force shows itself
among people in the West who regard themselves as
revolutionaries. The "new left" and all the various groups
that seek confrontation with present establishments and
work for radical change are not governed by a consistent
ideology so far as their goals and their long term strate-
gies are concerned. They are not attracted by the bureau-
cratic governments of Communist nations. They often ad-
mire guerrilla revolutionaries such as Castro, Mao-Tse-
tung and Che Guevara but it is the spirit and tactics of
these men that appeal to them rather than their pictures
of a new political and social order. These radical wes-
terners would be glad if it were possible to mount a
successful revolt against a government that wages an
immoral war in Vietnam, against a society that is controlled by white racism, against political parties that offer

no choice, and against a culture that is spiritually oppressive and morally corrupting and that provides no roles for these individuals which they regard as meaningful. Some of these criticisms of existing society may be exaggerated but my point is that the stance of those who take this line is not Communist in ideological inspiration, in direction or in organization. As Herbert Marcuse, one of its chief mentors, says, this radical "student movement contains a very strong element of anarchy." (*The New York Times Magazine*, October 27, 1968, p. 30.)

All that I have said calls for a complete revision of the attitude of Christians toward Communism and also of the attitudes which American Christians should have toward their government's policies in relation to Communist countries. Communism is no longer one entity; it is changeable; it is not the major reality even in the nations with Communist regimes. Our government's policies should differ from nation to nation. They should emphasize the importance of relationships of all kinds with every Communist nation, including China which is now being accepted as a reality and Cuba which is still kept under the rug. They should take account of the fear that both Russia and China have of our power and avoid provocative actions near their borders that we would not permit near our own borders. They should not be based on the assumption that Communist nations are now inspired by an aggressive revolutionary purpose that contains within it an indefinite threat to other nations. National imperialism may at times be a threat but it should be dealt with as such and not as though it called for a holy war against Communism. As we see revolutionary movements which have Communist inspiration or support in Asia or Africa or Latin America, we should not conjure up the old fear of a Communist monolith behind these developments and we should not seek to keep an American counter-revolutionary lid on them.[2]

In relation to Asian Communism, Professor Edwin Reischauer—who combines academic knowledge of Asia with the perceptions available to one who was for five years American ambassador to Tokyo—has come to be one of our wisest guides. His emphasis on the role of nationalism in Asia helps us to keep things in perspective. He writes:

> Thus in Asia, nationalism is the basic driving force and Communism the technique sometimes adopted to fulfill it. While one could say that Communism has exploited na-

---

[2] I think that there are three different approaches to a judgment about American policy in Vietnam and all lead to the same negative conclusion. The first is that the presuppositions of the policy are mistaken, especially those that are based upon the idea of the worldwide and unified Communist aggression that must be stopped in Vietnam or it will spread indefinitely. Also there has been the tendency to apply the Munich analogy and to assume that European precedents are helpful guides to what is possible for American power to do in Asia. The second is the realization that our government has tried to do what could not be done without destroying the nation that it sought to help. It has attempted by massive bombing in the South to impose the unpopular Saigon regime on the whole of South Vietnam, though this military action has proved to be self-defeating. As a foreign white military presence that takes the place of the French, our power has not been able to create in South Vietnam a national community. The third is the terrible human cost of the war both to the people of Vietnam and to our own people. The enormous American technological power to destroy is out of hand. The bombing and burning and maiming of hundreds of thousands of noncombatants and the turning of millions of helpless people into homeless refugees have been massive atrocities in themselves and no political objective could justify the sheer volume of this destruction and this imposed suffering. At last American opinion has caught up with the realities of this war and it is now commonplace to refer to it as the greatest mistake in American history.

tionalism, a truer description of the situation is that Communism in Asia is but one of nationalism's vehicles.

(*Beyond Vietnam*, Vintage Books, 1967, p. 64)

The nationalism of nations that surround China, including that of Vietnam, both North and South, is the best assurance of a pluralistic Asia in which China will inevitably have great influence but which need not be swallowed up in a Chinese Communist empire. The Soviet Union would be as much opposed to such Chinese domination as the United States. Nationalism creates its own problems and can inspire its own destructive zealots but at this moment in world history it does provide a brake on the extension of any form of ideological domination and it helps to protect the independence and freedom of peoples.

Nothing that I have said represents a guarantee of peace or freedom in the world. There are deep conflicts and some of them are enhanced by the ideological lenses through which people still see them. Scores of new, struggling nations which need governments strong enough to bring about radical social changes have not been able to establish them and so they drift to the edge of anarchy or they establish regimes that have no means of or no desire for realizing radical social goals. Revolutionary Communism of the Cuban type may succeed in establishing itself in some of these situations and this may be better for them than other actual alternatives and it is not for the United States to oppose it in favor of stagnation or some reactionary oligarchy. The world is and will continue to be disturbed for as long as we can see ahead, and in the United States we have our own need of radical change, in our cities and in the plight of our black citizens, with no sign of a comprehensive program to meet that need. I do not write this chapter in order to say that with the passing of the Communist monolith and with the passing of the Cold War, as it was known in the 1950's, life will be easier. Rather I am saying that we should avoid the old stereotypes and the old simplistic views of Communism so that we can see what the new problems are.

There is one new phase of the relation between Christianity and Communism which says a great deal to us: it is the dialogue between Christians and Communists, or Marxists, in several countries. Here I use the word "Marxist" to describe thinkers rather than political figures, though if they are really Marxists they cannot separate themselves from politics. In eastern Europe there has been a good deal of this dialogue in Czechoslovakia, Yugoslavia and Poland. Also there has been intensive dialogue in Italy and France with considerable interest in it among Christians in Germany. One of the most remarkable features of the dialogue is that Roman Catholics have taken a great deal of the initiative on the Christian side. One of the effects of the second Vatican Council was to change profoundly the attitude of Roman Catholics to Communists. Previously Roman Catholics have been leaders in a crusade against Communism on spiritual grounds. Communism was seen chiefly as atheistic and as the enemy of the Church. The present climate is remarkably different. Pope John XXIII in his encyclical *Pacem in Terris* gave a signal for this changed attitude and, especially in one paragraph (159), emphasized the difference between philosophical teachings and the movements that stem from them which are subject to historical changes. He did not mention Communism as such but his distinction is similar to mine between Communism as a system and changing contemporary nations with Communist regimes. The Church has not changed its mind about Communism as a system and especially about the Marxist-Leninist teachings which have provided its intellectual frame and yet deems it possible to discuss ultimate religious issues with a new breed of Communist thinkers.

If there were no such breed of Communists, the dialogue would not have much point and it is significant that there is no such dialogue between official Christians in the Soviet Union and official Communists. What Christian-Communist dialogue there is in the Soviet Union is underground. But in the nations that I have mentioned it is very much above ground. This new breed of Communists or Marxists are humanists who loathe the repressive spirit of official Communism in most countries with Communist regimes. They appeal from Stalinist party hacks and official ideologues to Karl Marx himself and especially to his early philosophical writings which show a grasp of the depth of the human person which is alien to totalitarian politics.[3] Also they emphasize a personal alienation of man from himself which Communist political systems have not in fact been able to overcome. The idea that the religious problems of man could be solved by new systems has been found illusory by a new generation of morally sensitive Communists. That they find a place on which to stand in Marx's own writings is most fortunate. As Professor Roszak says, "This emphasis on Marx's early writings may say more about them than about him."[4] Do we not all find correctives for the sys-

---

[3] Portions of these writings are published in Erich Fromm's *Marx's Concept of Man* (New York: Frederick Ungar Publishing Co.), 1961.

[4] *The Making of a Counter Culture* (New York: Anchor, 1969), p. 91.

tems under which we live by appealing to neglected writings of the founders or to neglected passages of Scripture? Existentialism, whether Christian or not, has kept raising the questions which orthodox Communism has treated as non-existent or as closed questions.

Fromm expresses this understanding of Marx's humanism when he says, "Marx's philosophy constitutes a spiritual existentialism in secular language."[5] He has edited a volume of essays by Marxist philosophers from many countries but especially from Yugoslavia, Czechoslovakia and Poland and these show how much ferment there is in Marxist circles created by the contrast between the humanistic correctives in Marx and the dehumanizing tendencies in totalitarian Communist systems.[6]

In the United States there are not many Communists or Marxists with whom Christians can have dialogue. Roman Catholic institutions have imported Professor Roger Garaudy several times recently for dialogue. Professor Garaudy is both an academic theoretician and a member of the Politbureau of the French Communist Party. His own view is that a society needs inspiration from both Christianity and Marxism. Professor Milan Machovec, a well-known Marxist philosopher from the Charles University in Prague, has recently visited this country under Protestant auspices and he has had a remarkable response from Christians in theological seminaries and universities. These encounters are merely the beginnings of a new relationship that will be established between Christians and Communists in many parts of the world. It may come late in the Soviet Union and later in China but religious questions, the existence of

---

[5] *Ibid.*, p. 5.

[6] Erich Fromm, *Socialist Humanism* (New York: Doubleday, 1965).

which are denied during the dogmatic and repressive period of Communism, will once again become open questions when that period passes, and the Christian ways of dealing with the questions, some of which I hope the reader will find in this book, will once again gain a hearing in Communist societies.

There is at least a hint of this new openness in a report of this dialogue between Christians and Marxists by Professor Jürgen Moltmann.[7] He writes of Marxist thinkers who "revised their well-known 'critique of religion' and asked for a new openness of men for transcendence." He quotes Professor Milan Prucha of the Prague Academy of Sciences, for example, who says: "Our Christian friends have awakened in us the courage for transcendence. For a long time we Marxists have tried to criticize and retard the Christian striving for transcendence. Should it not, rather, be our task to encourage the Christians to be even more radical in their striving for transcendence?" Moltmann also quotes Roger Garaudy (whom I have mentioned) as saying the following: "What would your (i.e., the Christian's) faith be like if it bore not in itself the latent atheism which prevents you from serving a false God? What would our atheism be like if it would not learn from your faith the transcendence of a God of whom we have no living experience?" This question doubtless comes in part from the felt need of a source of judgment from beyond the Communist party or the Communist society when these are informed by an orthodoxy that is a justification of party policy or of a new status quo in a nation. Something more is implied in a statement which Moltmann

---

[7] *Religion, Revolution, and the Future* (New York: Scribners, 1969), pp. 63-64.

quotes from Professor Machovec to the effect that "after the solution of the economic problems, the 'searching for the meaning of life' would become more and more the crucial problem of the future." Such a statement opens up a new horizon of religious and theological discovery which Christians and Communists can explore together.

Christians have intellectual problems of their own and are less likely to approach Communists with an "I told you so" attitude. Rather they should rejoice that there is this new opportunity to share with those who have been adversaries this search for better ways of expressing and relating to each other aspects of truth which those on each side have seen. One by-product of this sharing may be that the most fateful "dividing wall of hostility" in our time will be broken down.

1

The Point of View

THIS BOOK is written by one who believes that Communism as a faith and as a system of thought is a compound of half-truth and positive error, that Communism as a movement of power is a threat to essential forms of personal and political freedom, and that it is a responsibility of Christians to resist its extension in the world. On the other hand, this book is written by one who believes that the errors of Communism are in large part the result of the failure of Christians, and of Christian churches, to be true to the revolutionary implications of their own faith, that the effectiveness of Communism lies chiefly in the fact that it seems to offer the exploited and neglected peoples of the world what has been denied them by a civilization that has often regarded itself as Christian.

The reader will find two emphases in the book which, as I believe, belong together but which, most often, in public discussions of Communism are separated and made to characterize opposing bodies of opinion. This dual approach to Communism, on the one hand, emphasizes the obligation to resist it as an oppressive form of power and, on the other hand, acknowledges the validity of much that Communism represents as a strong reminder of the moral limitations of our own middle-class world and as a promised goal that meets the aspirations of millions of people who have been excluded from the benefits of that world. I hope that as they are developed in this book neither of these emphases will encourage the kind of illusion that hides the truth in the other. I hope to make it clear that this dual approach to Communism does not mean that one should call attention to both the good and the evil of Communism in such a way as to steer a middle course in relation to it. The good in its idealism and in its achievements makes it more effective and so more dangerous than a movement that can be shown to be rotten and cynical at its center.

The emphasis in this book upon Communism as a promise of a more just order of society and upon Communism as a corrective of the attitudes of the conventional Church, while not implying that it is any less important to resist the extension of Communism, does have an important bearing on the conditions and methods of resistance. If the judgments upon which this emphasis is based are correct, the extension of Communism cannot be prevented by negative propaganda governed by religious hostility or inspired by the beneficiaries of Western capitalism, nor can it be prevented primarily by military power. It can be prevented only by those who have a sounder faith and a better program to meet human needs and unsolved problems.

Communism has been strong where Christians and churches have often been weak, in providing a means of changing unjust institutions in the interests of their victims. Communism is weak in not foreseeing the extent of the new forms of oppression to which its own program gives rise, and this weakness, on the deepest level, is religious. Unconsciously it offers false solutions to religious problems, the existence of which it does not recognize. What that sentence means, and what the Christian solutions are to those same religious problems, will be the main subject of the chapters which follow.

2

The Nature of Communism

In ANY exposition of the nature of Communism one might concentrate on the teachings of Marx and Engels—the original source of Communism as a movement and as a system of thought; or one might concentrate on the contemporary institutions and policies of the Soviet Union, together with the behavior of Communist parties around the world. Either of these approaches, taken by itself, would constitute an evasion of the real problem of Communism. Communism as a contemporary movement is successful in convincing millions of people that it is the bearer of the Marxist dream for human society, of the promise of a new order more favorable to justice than the feudal or bourgeois societies which they know.

The institutions and policies of the Soviet Union are remote from this dream and promise, but there are explanations of this discrepancy that seem to satisfy most of those who feel strongly the attraction of Communism. The total impact of Communism today represents a combination of social promise and Russian power.[1] The observer is wise who is not dogmatic about the precise rela-

---

[1] It is necessary now to have in mind Chinese power also whenever Russian power is mentioned. Also, example today may be as important as power.

tionship between them. Indeed, the ways in which Russian power is used to serve the social promise, and the social promise is used to serve Russian power, in all probability vary from time to time, and motives are mixed on both sides of the Iron Curtain. It is enough for our purpose to acknowledge that both factors are present and that they are made to serve each other.

In what follows, I shall discuss Communism as "A Promise of a New Order," as "An Interpretation of Life," and as "A Revolutionary Method."

Communism as a Promise of a New Order

Modern Communism came into the world as a prophetic movement of protest against the human consequences of mid-nineteenth century capitalism. The *Communist Manifesto*, written by Marx and Engels one hundred years ago, contained most bitter descriptions of the condition of the laboring class and most confident affirmations of the self-destructive nature of the capitalistic system. It described the process by which the *bourgeoisie* were producing their own "gravediggers" and by which the revolution was being prepared within the womb of the old society that was rotten with injustice and unable to solve its own technical problems. It saw the root of the evil of society in the private ownership of property and announced that the theory of the Communists "may be summed up in a single sentence: abolition of private property." It gave a picture of the relationship between social classes according to which the world was divided into two classes, with the proletariat on the way to become the vast majority.

The *Manifesto* made no allowance for any possibility of improvement of the condition of the proletariat short of a complete economic and political revolution. It exaggerated the spiritual contrast between the classes as well as the inevitable increase in economic differences between them, for it assumed that it was true of the proletarian of 1848 that "law, morality, religion, are to him so many bourgeois prejudices, behind which lurk in ambush just as many bourgeois interests." It proclaimed that the revolution was imminent, that as the proletariat became the immense majority and as the crises of capitalism became more catastrophic, the workers would capture the machinery of the state and use its political power to effect the abolition of private property "to centralize all instruments of production in the hands of the state." It is an essential part of this view of society that political institutions have no independence of the economic struggle, that the "executive of the modern state is but a committee for managing the common affairs of the whole *bourgeoisie*," and that after the revolution the state will be "the proletariat organized as the ruling class."

This Communist vision of what ought to be and the Communist promise of what could be expected in the near future have, since 1848, given Communism its moral power in the world. It can be criticized as a quite inadequate forecast of developments under capitalism, with the rise of trade-unionism and the development of social legislation. It can be criticized as an oversimplification of the class structure, with its division of society into only two socially effective classes. It can be criticized for its complete neglect of the common patriotic, moral, and religious sentiments and convictions that have continued to hold the classes together in the very nations in which Communism was expected to come first. The development of a Fascist form of collectivism was not even imagined as a dread possibility. These and many more criticisms are suggested by events in western Europe and America since 1848, and yet the vision and the promise continue to be convincing to many millions of people who have never had a chance to share the prosperity of the middle-class world.

This vision and promise were translated into somewhat different terms by Lenin. He related them to his own dream of making Russia, an industrially backward nation, the first Communist state and to the situation created by the first world war, which he interpreted as an imperialist war that was the inevitable fruit of the rivalry of capitalist nations and which could be used to advance the cause of revolution. He also related them to his own emphasis upon the need for a disciplined party that would act as the leader of the proletariat and which was to be the real center of power in "the dictatorship of the proletariat." Perhaps most fatefully of all, he related them to the resentments and aspirations of the peoples who had been under colonial rule. They became for him a kind of international proletariat among which Communism has its greatest opportunity to win support.

Under his influence the first steps toward Communism were taken in a nation that had had no successful liberal revolution, that had had no experience of democracy or civil liberties as understood in western Europe and America. The vision and the promise persisted as factors in the dynamic behind the new Russian system; perhaps more important for our purpose, they continued to attract support for both Communism and the Soviet Union in other countries. I shall say more later about the ways in which this vision and this promise have been corrupted or obscured as a result of the Russian dictatorship, but here I want to emphasize the fact that they are still effective both within and outside the Soviet Union.

The promise of Communism is given substance by the actual achievements of the Soviet Union in economic planning, in the extraordinary rapid industrialization of the country, in the development of a new society where education and social services have been made available to a vast population, where the youth of all classes have a sense of participation in a great experiment, where the standard of life has been raised for the masses of the people, and where the fear of unemployment is unknown. The toughness of the Soviet society in war has been a test of the reality of some of these gains. The effectiveness of these achievements in reinforcing the Communist promise is undercut only to a limited extent by any answer that may be given to the question as to whether or not these gains have been offset by the human cost of the revolution and the dictatorship. There are so many explanations that can be given of the darker side of the Russian experiment—explanations that come from the history of Russia with its despotism and poverty, from the terrible burdens of war, from the foreign hostility to the Soviet experiment—that, as I have said, those who feel strongly the attraction of the Communist promise are not much troubled by this kind of question. Moreover, the estimate that one makes of the human cost of this experiment depends upon one's own historical situation, and the cost will be reckoned in minimum terms by all who have never had any experience of political or cultural freedom.

I shall now deal with three aspects of the promise of Communism.

First, it is assumed that the dictatorship will give way to a free society in which the coercive aspects of the state will no longer exist. The future society will have no police. The new order of freedom can be expected when the capitalistic institutions have been uprooted, when the remnants of capitalistic psychology have been overcome through a quite different kind of education and social conditioning, when no capitalistic nations will "encircle" the Soviet Union—when all need for military preparations will have disappeared. Lenin, at the time of the Russian Revolution and just before the establishment of his dictatorship, wrote an amazing prophecy of the coming of the ideal society that would be free from all compulsion. He said:

And then [after the resistance of the capitalists has been broken] will democracy itself begin to *wither away* due to the simple fact that, freed from capitalistic slavery, from the untold horrors, savageries, and infamies of capitalistic exploitation, people will gradually *become accustomed* to the observance of the elementary rules of social life that have been known for centuries and repeated for thousands of years in all school books; they will become accustomed to observing them without force, without compulsion, without subordination, without the special apparatus for compulsion which is called the state.[2]

This prophecy of the "withering away" of the "democratic" state that proletarian dictatorship is expected to produce must be taken in connection with the Marxist idea that the state is merely the instrument by which the ruling class keeps other classes in subjection. If the state is defined in this way and if the goal of a classless society is attained, then it is obvious that there need be no state. It is not denied that there will still have to be forms of

---

[2] *The State and Revolution,* Little Lenin Library, Vol. 14 (New York: International Publishers Co., 1932), p. 74.

administration in society but these will not require any coercive authority, for men are expected to live rationally, and freely to seek the common good when the modern root of all evil, the capitalistic form of property, is destroyed. This doctrine is one of the most optimistic conceptions of man ever held, for it finds the only obstacle to the good life in economic institutions that can be changed by a political and social revolution. I want to emphasize here the fact, to which I shall return later, that freedom constitutes no problem for Communist thought, for it is assumed that freedom will be realized inevitably as a by-product of a successful Communist revolution. This may well be the most fateful error of judgment that the Communists have made.

Stalin has always regarded himself as a faithful follower of Lenin. What does he say about the continuation of dictatorship? In his report to the Eighteenth Party Congress in 1939 he explained that the state may still be necessary for a long time because of "capitalistic encirclement." In case of a change in the situation abroad, he said of the state: "No, it will not remain and will atrophy if the capitalistic encirclement is liquidated and a socialistic encirclement takes its place."[3]

This suggests the usual explanation of the continuation of dictatorship offered by apologists for the Soviet Union. The pressure from the other powers, from 1917 until Russia was victorious in the second world war, has been a real factor in determining events in Russia. It has necessitated military preparations and it did encourage internal opposition to the regime. Today, fears of the capitalistic powers remain and they can still be used as an

[3] Joseph Stalin, *Leninism: Selected Writings* (New York: International Publishers Co., 1942), p. 474.

explanation of the need for armaments and dictatorship. Americans may believe that there is no real threat to Russia from outside today, but both Communist dogma about the inevitability of a final attempt of the capitalistic world to seek to destroy the revolution and the bitter experience of Russia from the revolution to the days of Munich and beyond have made her naturally suspicious of the Western nations.[4] This suspicion is confirmed in Russian eyes today by much reckless talk on the part of Americans who interpret the struggle between East and West primarily in military terms. It would be difficult to assess the extent to which this fear of the outside world is the cause of the persistence of dictatorship in comparison with the tendency of all who hold absolute power to perpetuate their power and in comparison with the Russian lack of experience of the conditions of political freedom.

Professor Eduard Heimann explains the persistence of dictatorship in terms of the unripeness of Russia for Communism. It had been the Marxist expectation that the revolution would come in nations in which industry was already organized in a relatively few large units and the people were unified through "the collectivized pattern of dependent work." In such a situation the self-conscious proletariat would be the immense majority and they could effect a transfer of power with a minimum of violence. But under Russian conditions, as Professor Heimann says: "The transition became more difficult; the dictatorship became a minority dictatorship rather than a majority dictatorship and consequently more violent and long-lived." He adds: "A dictatorship, however nec-

---

[4] See discussion of this Russian fear in its relation to most recent developments on pages 166–167.

essary for objective reasons, is a formidable vested interest and will not be slow in rationalizing its abuses by reference to its objective necessity."[5] This last observation, which is so important from the Christian point of view, lies outside Communist calculations about human nature.

A second element in the Communist promise is the belief that when society moves from the preliminary stage that is identified with "socialism," which is governed by the principle that all should be rewarded according to their *contribution*, to Communism, it will be possible to realize the ideal of the distribution of income according to *need*. The Soviet Union at present is said to be in the socialist stage. (This use of the word "socialism" would be rejected by all Western democratic socialists.) There are admitted differences of income in accordance with the contribution made by workers or professional people or government officials or artists to Soviet society. The Soviet Union is still controlled by the fact of scarcity, and the need of economic incentives for productivity is recognized. But it is assumed that in the future all existing inequalities and class distinctions will be wiped out. The same optimism about the future prevails here as in the case of the withering away of the dictatorship. Stalin, in an address in 1935 to the Stakhanovites who ironically were working under the pressure of speed-up techniques, gives a picture of this better future. After explaining that socialism is a society in which income is distributed according to work performed, he describes Communism as follows:

[5] Eduard Heimann, *Freedom and Order* (New York: Charles Scribner's Sons, 1947), p. 153.

Communism represents a higher stage of development. The principle of Communism is that in a Communist society each works according to his abilities and receives articles of consumption, not according to the work he performs, but according to his needs as a culturally developed individual. This means that the cultural and technical level of the working class has become high enough to undermine the basis of distinction between mental labor and manual labor, that the distinction between mental and manual labor has already disappeared, and that productivity of labor has reached such a high level that it can provide an absolute abundance of articles of consumption, and as a result society is able to distribute these articles in accordance with the needs of its members.[6]

Notice that it is assumed by Stalin that the fact of abundance itself will make it possible to overcome inequalities. Acquisitiveness will no longer tempt men to seek to possess more than their neighbors because everyone will have enough in any case to satisfy both material and cultural needs. It is taken for granted that in this Communist utopia the problem of incentive will be fully solved.

There is a third element in the Communist promise that has a great appeal especially in Asia and Africa. It is the promise of a society in which all imperialistic exploitation will be a thing of the past and in which the humiliating discrimination from which the colored races suffer will be done away. Here the contrast between the Communist promise and Russian policy, on the one hand, with the practices of the Anglo-Saxon nations especially, on the other, is such that it is natural for many millions of people, including some Christians, among the colored

---

[6] *Leninism: Selected Writings,* p. 368.

races to feel that Communism holds out more hope for them than Western democracy which has been so untrue to its own principles as it has come into contact with the colored races. Russian policy in dealing with racial minorities in the Soviet Union has always been a strong point in favor of Communism.

The Communist analysis of imperialism, according to which it is an inevitable expression of advanced capitalism and according to which it will as inevitably be abandoned by a Communist state, is the intellectual background for this openness to Communism among the victims of the older imperialism. It seems that forms of Russian or Communist expansion are, by definition, something different from "imperialism" but there are many people in the path of that expansion to whom this verbal exercise is full of bitter irony.[7]

It should be said here that one momentous difference between Communism and National Socialism lies in the fact that the opponents of Communism do not have upon them the indelible mark of race. It is often said that the Communists put class where the Nazis put race, but this is a misleading comparison because classes are changing historical phenomena whereas racial differences are for all practical purposes permanent. Since the opponents of Communism are defined in political and economic terms, a changed historical situation may well cause Communists to be tolerant and co-operative in dealing with those who are now regarded as "class enemies." Thus

---

[7] In Asia the assumption has been widely held that since imperialism as Asians knew it developed with capitalism, a nation that is not capitalistic will not be imperialistic. Confidence that this is so is wearing thin, partly because of the experience of Hungary but even more because of the dealing of China with Tibet and her behavior on the borders of India.

there is always the possibility of living with Communists without being the permanent objects of their hostility. In the case of National Socialists, no such possibility existed for those who were regarded by them as belonging to inferior races.

It is the Communist theory that the proletariat as a class is the representative of the true interests of society as a whole. As Marx has explained it: "The class making a revolution appears from the very start, merely because it is opposed to a *class*, not as a class but as the representative of the whole of society; it appears as the whole mass of society confronting the one ruling class."[8] This presupposes the expectation that the "ruling class" will become smaller and smaller and increasingly parasitic, so that it ceases to represent any real part of the general welfare.

Communism as an Interpretation of Life

Communism is a total philosophy of life. It develops authoritative answers to more questions than Christianity, especially Protestant Christianity. There is a Communist interpretation of history which is a guide to revolutionary strategy. This interpretation of history is supported by a metaphysic which has been developed in contrast to philosophies that are idealistic in the broad sense that they regard mind as prior to matter, and which is in reaction against all forms of religion, especially Christianity. This metaphysic, "dialectical materialism," should be understood by Christian critics of Communism as a fighting creed. It is a creed that drives men to change the structures of social life, rather than to rationalize them either

---

8 Karl Marx, *The German Ideology* (New York: International Publishers Co.), p. 41.

by identifying the ideal with the real in terms of concrete historical institutions or by piously accepting the existing order, however unjust it may be, as ordained by God.

Dialectical materialism is a philosophical support for the materialistic interpretation of history, according to which the primary factors in all historical developments are the forms of ownership and production. This economic interpretation of history has left space for the recognition of the effectiveness of the purpose of men to bring about the new order, but it remains a one-sided view of life. Any positive value that it has comes from the fact that it has been a corrective of one-sided spiritualistic conceptions of life that have been dominant both in the Church and in polite society—spiritualistic conceptions of life which mask the destructive effects of economic institutions upon spiritual values.

The worst of all combinations of ideas and attitudes in this connection is the use of spiritual philosophies of life to encourage the economically poor to accept their lot without complaint, while those who hold those spiritual philosophies take for granted their own economic privileges. Against all such tendencies Marxism, even at its crudest, is a valid protest. As the late Nicolas Berdyaev has said: "The question of bread for myself is a material question, but the question of bread for my neighbors, for everybody, is a spiritual and a religious question."[9]

This philosophy of dialectical materialism is combined with atheism. In itself it is no more atheistic than any naturalistic philosophy that accepts the experienced world of nature and history as self-sufficient, but it is

---

[9] Nicolas Berdyaev, *Origin of Russian Communism* (New York: Charles Scribner's Sons, 1937), p. 225.

accompanied by a bitter polemic against all theistic religion. To some extent this is the result of a narrowly conceived scientific view of the world, and to some extent the Communist philosophy itself is a rationalization of a strong antireligious feeling. I shall reserve discussion of Communist attitudes toward religion until later. Meanwhile it is enough to say that even if there were no antireligious feeling and even if no reasons based upon social experience could be alleged for discrediting all forms of theistic religion, the philosophical system known as dialectical materialism has no place for faith in God as the Creator on whom the whole experienced world of nature and history depends. If there are religious elements implicit in Communism, as I shall maintain at a later point, they take the form of devotion to human goals and trust in a historical process with no god other than the process.

There are several common misunderstandings of Communist teaching that Christians should learn to avoid. There is a danger that they may concentrate on a caricature of Communism and thus miss the corrective that is in it, and there is a further danger that they may celebrate a premature victory over the caricature and thus fail to discern the deeper issues that divide Christianity and Communism. I shall now emphasize some of the things that Communism is not.

Communist materialism is not a mechanistic form of materialism or one that leaves no room for any of the higher spiritual or cultural values. Indeed, it would probably be less misleading to think of dialectical materialism as a form of monistic naturalism. The word "materialism" is an emotional word that often causes critics of Communism to become excited at the wrong point. There is a famous sentence of William Temple's that needs to be remembered when this word is used. He says that "Christianity is the most materialistic religion in the world."[10] By this he means that Christianity emphasizes the created world in which what we call matter has sacramental meaning; the close relation between body and spirit; man's need of bread and of the material conditions of life; and at the center of it all there is the emphasis upon the Word made *flesh*. Communism, with its materialism, is a one-sided and truncated philosophy but it is doubtful if it is more misleading, even from the Christian point of view, than philosophies or religious attitudes which neglect the material basis of life.

It may eliminate some of the self-righteous emotion, which Americans are often tempted to feel when they think of Communist "materialism," to realize two things about our own culture. One is the very great element of practical materialism in our national life. This has distorted our own culture so that in large measure our standards of success are materialistic and our goals for living are materialistic in contrast to our professed ideals. Also, on the intellectual side there is among us a very widespread "scientism" (to be distinguished from science, which as such does not have these pretentions)—the faith that science and technology provide all that men need to know and all the resources that are required for the salvation of man and society. The Communists who have been able to be planners and builders rather than conspirators and revolutionaries develop a kind of "scientism" that would not be much out of place in some American universities where the religious negations of philo-

---

[10] William Temple, *Nature, Man, and God* (New York: The Macmillan Co., 1934), p. 478.

sophical naturalism and faith in science form the philosophy of life of many professors and students.

Communist materialism is not fatalistic. On the contrary, it has been a stimulus to action. Moreover, Communist movements depend to a considerable extent upon the leadership of those who are attracted by its social purpose, who are themselves moved by moral conviction. Marx and Lenin were supreme examples of this. There is a very confused relationship between determinism and freedom in Communist thought and also in some forms of Christian theology. It is true that Communism does not recognize explicitly enough the capacity of men to be moved by non-material or non-economic factors in life and that it does not understand the full implications of the freedom of the human spirit to make history, which Communists themselves often exemplify. But it is misleading to make this criticism of Communism a ground for accusing it of denying all human freedom. Engels opens the door to a significant form of freedom when he says: "Freedom of the will therefore means nothing but the capacity to make decisions with real knowledge of the subject," or again when he says: "Freedom therefore consists in the control over ourselves and over external nature which is founded on knowledge of natural necessity; it is therefore necessarily a product of historical development."[11]

It has often been noted that there is a parallel here between Communist thought and practice and Calvinistic thought and practice. In both cases there is a doctrine that seems to be a hard determinism. In both cases this doctrine became a fighting creed and a great stimulus to

---

[11] *Anti-Duhring*, translated by Emile Burns (New York: International Publishers Co., 1936), p. 105.

action. In both cases the doctrine has failed to undercut the tendency to moral condemnation of opponents, which presupposes their moral responsibility. In Christian thought there is a tendency to oscillate between a one-sided emphasis upon human freedom and a one-sided determinism, but the practical attitudes of Christians make room for both elements. There is a paradoxical relationship between the realities that underlie our theories about the problem of freedom versus determinism that easily becomes a stumbling block to thinkers, whether they are Christian or Communist.

Communism is not a form of moral cynicism. I say this in spite of the fact that Communism has been one of the factors in dissolving the moral assumptions of modern man. On one level Communist tactics have been based on pure expediency; they have encouraged cynicism about all political methods, and they have used ideas chiefly as weapons in the class struggle. On a deeper level the Communist criticism of "bourgeois ethics" and of all absolute ethics has encouraged a skeptical attitude toward all moral standards. The opponents of Communism have not discouraged the idea that it is unmoral, but they are mistaken.

The ethical relativism of classical Marxism is a weapon in the struggle against the moral pretensions of the bourgeois class with which Communism is at war. Ethical absolutes, as interpreted by Christians and by the whole respectable world, were slanted in favor of the *status quo*. Engels brings this out very clearly in his *Anti-Duhring*. After showing how moralists have claimed for their standards the same objectivity as attaches to mathematical propositions, or to the fact that Napoleon died on May 5, 1821, he goes on to show that these objective "eternal truths" are used by classes to defend their interests. He is driven to a quite one-sided view of the origin of morality, but the following passage shows that he is not as relativistic as his main argument implies:

> And as society has hitherto moved in class antagonisms, morality was always a class morality; it has hitherto justified the domination and the interests of the ruling class, or, as soon as the oppressed class has become powerful enough, it has represented the revolt against this domination and the future interests of the oppressed. That in this process there has on the whole been progress in morality, as in all other branches of human knowledge, cannot be doubted. But we have not yet passed beyond class morality. A really human morality which transcends class antagonisms and their legacies in thought becomes possible only at a stage of society which has not only overcome class contradictions but has even forgotten them in practical life.[12]

Those words, obviously, give away the case for complete moral relativism, for the reference to progress in morality presupposes a *standard* of progress and the whole outlook is controlled by the possibility of a "really human morality" that is to come after the revolution in a classless society.

The whole Communist attack upon capitalistic society is ethical through and through. This comes out in the technical discussions of surplus value in *Capital* and in the highly emotional exhortations of the *Communist Manifesto*. It is apparent in the motives that cause individuals to become Communists, that cause many of them to sacrifice their own personal privileges and to endure all manner of hardships and persecutions. Motives are mixed in all of us and Communism can be an expression

---

[12] *Ibid.*, p. 105.

of sheer personal rebellion and of hatred, but its great leaders often are driven by an outraged sense of justice of which one of the by-products may be hatred. Lenin's own life was changed in his youth by the hanging of his brother by the Russian government, and often it is some such experience of great wrong in the old order that generates both devotion to what is believed to be a just cause and a hard and hostile attitude toward the whole class that is held responsible for wrongs done.

In spite of the fact that *Christian* ethics is one of the main targets of Communist attack in the criticism of all ethics in terms of ideology, there is more in common between Christianity and Communism here than appears on the surface. I am using "ideology" here in the technical sense that refers to systems of thought that are developed to defend the interest and bias of a particular social group. I have emphasized the fact that Communist relativism is a weapon in the struggle against the old order rather than a theory that is all-inclusive, and that actually the Communists are not thoroughgoing ethical relativists. But they see through the pretensions of everyone except themselves. Engels describes the typical moralist as a prophet who proves that all of his predecessors were wrong but that he "has in his bag, all ready made, final and ultimate truth, eternal morality, and eternal justice." Engels adds that "this has all happened so many hundreds and thousands of times that we can only feel astonished that there should still be people credulous enough to believe this, not of others, but of themselves."[13] We may add that it was to happen once again, for Communism was to provide its final answers to the central human problems.

---

[13] *Anti-Duhring*, p. 245.

Engels was quite right in thinking that the Church has often absolutized a system of social morality conditioned by class interests and that its teaching has been used as a support for the established order. This is a form of universal human sin, of the tendency to see the world from one's own limited point of view without recognizing its limitations. Christians are not free from this sin, but they should be prepared by their understanding of human nature to guard against it in themselves. There is an absolute Christian ethic, and the problem of relating it to concrete human actions is one of the central issues of contemporary Christian thought. But one condition for relating it rightly to our concrete decisions is to take seriously the Communist ideological criticism of most ways of doing it. The distortion of our ethical judgments by the almost unconscious assumptions of our nation or class is so great that Christians need to use the criticism of the early Marxists as a kind of purgative. At this point they will not be helped much by contemporary Communism because, in the interests of some distant goal, it has moved beyond the stage of criticism of the *status quo*. It is now preoccupied with the task of discrediting the ideals and institutions of its opponents in order to defend the ideals and institutions of the Soviet Union which for them occupy the position of a new *status quo*. The degree of Communist self-righteousness in doing so, it would be difficult to surpass.

I have already quoted the extraordinary statement by Lenin concerning the future society after the withering away of the state. One of the interesting elements in that passage is the conventional character of the morality that is projected upon the distant future. Lenin says: "People will gradually *become accustomed* to the observance of the elementary rules of social life that have been known for centuries and repeated for thousands of years in all school books." Put beside that prophecy the actual moral precepts that are incorporated in Soviet education according to the pedagogical textbook that was published under the title *I Want to be Like Stalin*.[14] There is dangerous nationalism in this book chiefly in the form of provincialism, for Russia seems to be almost the whole world, and there is foolish adulation of Stalin and there is much authoritarianism in educational method and in the attitude toward the state, but notice the following passages:

> Sometimes, for example, the older children bully the younger, the physically strong taunt the weak, boys treat girls scornfully and occasionally even insult them, children with certain defects, such as stuttering or some physical disability, may be teased or ridiculed. All such forms of behavior are vestiges from the old society and the old life. (p. 76)

> The pupil in our schools must be incapable, because of his inner strength and inherent honesty, of telling a lie. . . . One must *be* honest, conscientious, truthful, and studious, and not merely *seem* to be such. (p. 79)

> The "Rules" require of the pupil of the Soviet school attentiveness to and consideration of the sick, the weak, the aged, and little children; also care of younger brothers and sisters. (p. 98)

If this book does indicate the kind of "new man" that the Soviet system of education is trying to develop, emphasis upon scrupulous honesty and upon the more tender virtues is most significant. It is in line with this same tendency that the development in Russia for the past

---

[14] Translated by Counts and Lodge (New York: The John Day Co., 1947).

decade or more has been in the direction of the discipline of the sexual life and the encouragement of family stability.[15]

We can obtain another view of Communism as an interpretation of life if we consider the relation between Communism and religion, including both the attitude of Communists toward historical forms of religion and the religious elements that are implicit in Communism.

The theoretical rejection of all forms of historical religion by Communists is complete. Religion is rejected as prescientific superstition. Religion is rejected as a support for social reaction, as an opiate of the people that turns their attention away from the revolutionary task of changing social institutions in this world. Religion is rejected as having no function at all after the Communist order has been fully established. Since it is regarded as humanity's way of escaping from the evils that are caused by all previous social systems, it can be expected to wither away when the Communist society has overcome the evils which create the need for such an escape. These criticisms of religion have been applied by the Russian Communists to religion in Russia, but it is a great mistake to assume that they are merely a reaction against the Russian Orthodox Church which, before the Russian Revolution, was in large measure an instrument of political and social oppression.   Marx and Engels gained their impression of religion from Roman Catholi-

---

[15] Soviet education has drawn much favorable comment even from Americans who are severe critics of the Communist system. It is significant that a recent study of Soviet education by a United States mission headed by the Commissioner of Education, Dr. Lawrence G. Derthick, emphasized as one of the favorable aspects of Soviet education its encouragement of "dignity and respect between boys and girls." *New York Times*, September 6, 1959, Sec. I, p. 43.

cism and Protestantism in western Europe. The Communist rejection of religion in general is as thoroughgoing as it can be, though there may be a peculiar degree of emotional revulsion against religion among Russian Communists. Lenin has given us his ideas about religion in unrestrained language. He sees the roots of all modern religion in capitalistic oppression. He says:

> The roots of modern religion are deeply embedded in the social oppression of the working masses, and in their complete helplessness before the blind forces of capitalism, which every day and every hour cause a thousand times more horrible suffering and torture for ordinary working folk than are caused by exceptional events such as war, earthquakes, etc. "Fear created the gods." Fear of the blind forces of capital—blind because its action cannot be foreseen by the masses—a force which at every step in life threatens the worker and the small businessman with "sudden," "unexpected," "accidental" destruction and ruin, bringing in their train beggary, pauperism, prostitution, and deaths from starvation—this is the taproot of modern religion which, first of all and above all, the materialist must keep in mind, if he does not wish to remain stuck forever in the kindergarten of materialism.[16]

Lenin assumes that religion is purely obscurantist and that both scientific enlightenment and a social order free from oppression will undermine it. He takes for granted that the working class can be relied upon to be antireligious and atheistic. He says: "The class conscious worker of today, brought up in big industry, and enlightened by town life, rejects religious prejudice with contempt." Lenin's opposition extends even to new forms of religion that were developed by sympathizers with

---

[16] *Religion*, pamphlet in Little Lenin Library, Vol. 7 (New York: International Publishers Co.), pp. 14–15.

Communism. Maxim Gorky had been interested in a new religious movement that resembled what we call in America non-theistic humanism, and it was oriented toward the spiritual support of the revolution, but even this Lenin dismissed with contempt. Any form of spiritual faith that broke with the negations of dialectical materialism was regarded as an entering wedge for the reactionary forms of idealism and religion against which all Communist thought is a violent protest.

I shall not attempt at this stage to criticize this conception of religion. My discussion of Christianity in the next chapters will be an attempt to show how abysmal the Communist misunderstanding of Christianity is, though it is not for Christians to cast stones at the Communists for this misunderstanding, for the Christian churches are largely responsible for it. Deeper than any misunderstanding of Christianity is the Communist failure to recognize the deeper levels of life, the permanent forms of sin and tragedy. Much more will be said about this later.

It is often said that Communism, whatever its representatives may think about religion, is itself a religion. This is of course denied violently by Communists themselves. To some extent it is a verbal matter. If the word "religion" is reserved for attitudes and movements which explicitly recognize dependence upon superhuman spiritual beings, it of course does not apply. But if religion is defined as man's relationship to whatever he regards as ultimate or to whatever he trusts most for deliverance from the evils and hazards of life, then Communism is undoubtedly religious. If one desires to avoid argument on the use of the word it is certainly true to say that Communism occupies the place in life for the convinced Communist that religions occupy in the lives of their

adherents. Communism offers a goal for life. It offers a
faith in redemption from all recognized evils. It offers an
interpretation of life's meaning which may be short-
sighted and one-sided but which at least does provide
the kind of guidance that the religious believer secures
from his doctrine. It even offers the kind of authority that
the more authoritarian churches provide for their members. Many other features of religion, such as sacred
scriptures and saints, have their analogues in Communism. The Communist, like the Christian and the ad-
herent of any of the higher religions, is a man of faith.
He is committed to a cause and he has an ultimate confidence that the highest powers, the existence of which
he will admit, are on the side of that cause.

Before concluding this discussion of Communism as an
interpretation of life it would be well to call attention to
the fact that, inadequate as it is from the Christian point
of view, Communism does offer many of our contemporaries a unified philosophy of life that makes more sense
to them than any that they have encountered. There is a
craving for such a total view of life and especially one
that unites for the believer thought and action. Communism provides a system of thought that is illuminating as
far as some areas of our life are concerned, and it offers a
plan of action as well. When this scheme of thought and
action is seen against the background of the contradictions of Western society—contradictions between the
Christian and democratic standards and the dominant
ways of life in nations that claim to be democratic and
in churches that claim to be Christian—it is not strange
that Communism has a strong appeal. The darker side of
Communism—its ruthless methods during the period of
revolution, and the dictatorship which is all that has yet
appeared anywhere as the result of revolution—can be

accepted by the Communist as a passing phase that
will be justified by what is still to come. To that darker
side of Communism we shall now turn.

Communism as a Revolutionary Method

We move into quite a different area when we consider
the methods used by Communists and defended by them
in principle during the period of the revolution and of
the dictatorship that follows. That period has not ended
in Russia or in any country where Communists have
power. The pattern of Communist policy is complex because the whole international conflict between the Soviet
Union and the Western democracies is closely related
to the struggle to maintain and extend the results of the
revolution in Russia.

It is in the midst of this revolutionary struggle that
the only ethical test that is recognized is whether or not
a given policy or action serves the Communist cause.
This is the hardest ethical problem raised by Communism. The problem is the same whether we see it in
terms of the treatment of political prisoners in Siberian
labor camps or whether we see it in terms of the dis-
honest tactics of American Communists in a labor union
or a student front organization.[17] The essential element
in both situations is that the opponents of Communism
are obstacles to be removed or neutralized rather than
persons to be respected and loved and redeemed for their
own sake.

There is a vast literature about the ethics of Communism during the revolutionary period, much of it written
by disillusioned Communists, and in detail it is hard to

---

[17] The references here are chiefly to an earlier period, especially
to the 1930's.

evaluate the evidence presented. It is safe to say that there are enough points that are not in dispute to, make the ethical issue quite clear in principle. Communism, as it touches political opponents, uses tactics of deception and methods of terror.

Professor Harold Laski, who has usually given Communism the benefit of any doubt, wrote in 1947 a pamphlet in which he gave the following description of Communist practice:

> The Communist parties outside Russia act without moral scruples, intrigue without any sense of shame, are utterly careless of truth, sacrifice without any hesitation the means they use to the ends they serve. . . . The only rule to which the Communist gives unswerving loyalty is the rule that a success gained is a method justified. The result is a corruption of both the mind and heart, which is alike contemptuous of reason and careless of truth.[18]

Let me give one illustration of Communist ruthlessness as it appears to Stalin and as it appears to a historian who is quite sympathetic with Russian policy. Stalin in 1931, in an article in *Pravda,* discusses the kulaks. He writes as follows:

> The kulak is an enemy of the Soviet government. There is not and cannot be peace between him and us. Our policy toward the kulaks is to eliminate them as a class. That, of course, does not mean that we can eliminate them at one stroke. But it does mean that we shall proceed in such a way as to surround them and eliminate them.

Then he gives emotional support for this policy by quoting Lenin. This quotation has the effect of destroying

---

[18] Quoted by Dr. J. H. Oldham from the pamphlet *The Steep Places,* in "The Church and the Disorder of Society," *Christendom,* Summer, 1948, p. 310.

any moral claim to be human on the part of the kulaks. Lenin had said:

> The kulaks are the most brutal, callous, and savage exploiters. . . . These bloodsuckers have grown rich on the want suffered by the people in the war. . . . These spiders have grown fat at the expense of the peasants who have been ruined by the war, at the expense of the hungry workers. These leeches sucked the blood of the toilers. . . . These vampires have been gathering the landed estates into their hands; they keep on enslaving the poor peasant.[19]

Now consider the human consequences of this policy of "eliminating the kulaks as a class." Professor Frederick L. Schuman, who cannot be accused of prejudice against the Soviet Union, describes the result of the war against the kulaks in connection with the great "famine" in the Ukraine in 1932–33. He says:

> Most of the victims, the number of whom cannot be ascertained in the absence of any official or accurate information, were kulaks who had refused to sow their fields or had destroyed their crops. Observation in the villages suggests that this portion of the peasantry was left to starve by the authorities and the collective farmers as a more or less deliberate policy. Large numbers (again unspecified) were deported to labor camps where some died of malnutrition and disease and others were rehabilitated into useful citizens. The human cost of "class war in the villages" was horrible and heavy. *The Party appeared less disturbed by dead kulaks than by dead cows.* [Italics mine.] The former were "class enemies."[20]

This illustration is typical of the Communist dealing with opponents. The same process is carried on against

---

[19] *Leninism: Selected Writings*, pp. 190-191.
[20] Frederick L. Schuman, *Soviet Politics* (New York: Alfred A. Knopf, Inc., 1946), p. 219.

any group of people who are judged to be "class enemies." They may be purged Russian Communists as in
the period of the great purge. They may be Social Democrats in eastern Germany. They may be the members of
any opposition party in Poland or Rumania or other
Balkan countries, or now in Czechoslovakia. Sudden
disappearance of some suspected individual, torture to
extract information, transportation to a forced labor
camp in the north where the victim may die of exposure
and hunger and leave no trace—this fate may await
anyone who is not careful to avoid suspicion.

Joseph Alsop, a correspondent of the *New York Herald
Tribune,* described from Berlin in 1947 the nature of the
Soviet terror in eastern Germany. His account of the
methods of interrogation that were used with anti-Communist Social Democrats is characteristic of the whole
literature concerning Nazi methods as well as Communist
methods of dealing with political prisoners. He follows
up the story of one German who, after three months of
torture and questioning, was sent to one of the old Nazi
concentration camps, Sachsenhausen. Of this camp he
says: "The place was the same as in the old days, except
that there were no gas chambers or death ovens. The
Soviet terror is certainly more ruthless than the terror
of the Nazis, but differs from it, at least, in this respect."
He then describes the methods used at Sachsenhausen:

At Sachsenhausen thirty-five to forty prisoners died daily,
many of them under punishment. Three classes of punishment were used. The lightest was the "Kra'zer"—solitary
confinement without food. Medium punishment was the
"bunker"—being placed in an open hole in the ground
from fifteen to twenty-five feet deep where offenders had
to "stand in their own filth" for ten or fifteen days. Most
of those who experienced the "bunker" died before re-

lease. Yet the punishment for the worst offenders was not the "bunker" but being sent to the M.V.D.'s labor camps in the Soviet Union.[21]

Estimates concerning the number of such victims in forced labor camps cannot be checked. Dallin and Nicolaevsky, in their book *Forced Labor in Soviet Russia*,[22] say that there are between 7,000,000 and 12,000,000 (p. 86) of them. These authors are said to be biased by writers who, on the other side, tend to whitewash the Soviet Union. Their book, however, is a deeply disturbing one. Even though the figures that they give may be too high, it is difficult to doubt that there are millions of persons who have had the experiences recorded in that book. The deliberate sentencing of persons to hopelessness and a living death for political reasons and the use of every available method to demoralize them as human beings, tempting them to betray one another for the sake of a little more food—this whole method, whether it be applied to two million or twenty million, creates the greatest moral difficulty. The practice of torturing persons in order to make them act against their consciences and thus to destroy their moral integrity is the most repellent element in the methods of Communists when they are in power. As one who has no interest in believing the worst about the Soviet Union, I find myself quite convinced by the conclusion that Dallin and Nicolaevsky draw from their data:

Each day [in a labor camp] is a struggle for bare existence, and those win out who have no moral scruples. This produces a general view among the prisoners that there is room in life only for those who are not troubled by virtue.[23]

---

[21] *New York Herald Tribune*, November 19, 1947.

[22] New Haven: Yale University Press, 1947.

[23] *Ibid.*, p. 19.

Lenin's wife, Krupskaya, discerned the moral conse-quence of all methods of political terrorism. When in 1908 Lenin, as his biographer says, "half in jest," told how he would stand up the opponents of revolution against the wall, his wife replied: "Yes, and you'll shoot precisely those that are better men for having the cour-age to express their views."[24]

Perhaps the most vicious feature of this whole method of forced labor is that it has been integrated into the productive system of the Soviet Union; so that there is an economic incentive to perpetuate it and even to in-crease the number of laborers. In a review of the book by Dallin and Nicolaevsky in *The New Statesman and Nation* (May 15, 1948), a journal that has usually given the benefit of the doubt to the Soviet Union, Edward Crankshaw, himself the author of an extraordinarily fair book about Russia, *Russia and the Russians,* makes this judgment about the system of forced labor in that country: "Since 1931 forced labor in the U.S.S.R. has not been comparable with penal servitude as generally un-derstood but has resembled in principle the slavery of vanished empires." It is indeed quite staggering to find that a movement that began with the honest purpose to liberate humanity from all forms of oppression should have come to accept a method of dealing with human beings that is more reactionary than any policy that is officially sanctioned by the nations that are supposed to represent the old capitalistic order.

One other phase of the dictatorship that should be mentioned here is its assumption that it should regiment every phase of culture. It is not surprising that phi-

---

[24] David Shub, *Lenin* (Garden City, N. Y.: Doubleday & Com-pany, 1948), p. 303.

losophers and economists who come into conflict with
official doctrine are demoted and silenced. But it shows
how thoroughgoing this cultural control is when even
musicians find themselves in the same situation. The
apologies of the Russian composer, Shostakovich, illustrate the pervasiveness of the dictatorship. After some
of his musical compositions were condemned as showing
traces of bourgeois influence, he said: "I know that the
party is right, that the party wishes me well, and that
I must search and find concrete creative roads which will
lead me toward a realistic Soviet people's art."[25]

Berdyaev, who has always preserved a remarkable de-
tachment from the usual criticisms of Communism in
the West, says of the Communist authorities that while
in political matters they show the capacity for "great
pliancy," in spiritual matters they are uncompromising.
He says: "But there is a domain in which Communism is
changeless, pitiless, fanatical, and in which it will grant
no concessions whatever. That is the domain of 'world
outlook,' of philosophy and consequently of religion also.
. . . It sometimes looks as though the Soviet government
would rather go on to the restoration of capitalism in
economic life than to granting freedom of conscience,
freedom of philosophic thought, freedom to create a
spiritual culture."[26]

The dictatorship of the proletariat that Marx thought
of as a brief interlude during which the many would
have to put the few in their place, an interlude that
would be followed by the abolition of the supremacy of
the proletariat itself as a class, has now been in power

---

[25] From a dispatch from Moscow, signed by Joseph Newman, in
the *New York Herald Tribune*, April 26, 1948.

[26] *Origin of Russian Communism*, pp. 205, 206.

for more than a generation. Communist idealism concerning the future has been very largely overshadowed by the grim realities of this dictatorship. Communist dictatorship seems to follow the laws of other dictatorships, and the insecurity of the ruling group forces it to deal ruthlessly with all signs of opposition. The consequence is that the almost inevitable terror that accompanies revolution is developed into a political system. The only moral criterion comes to be whether or not a policy serves the dictatorship. The idealism of Communism becomes a support for any such policy. It can be sincerely argued by any defender of Communism that the ideal goal to which it promises to bring the world is worth any cost. If at the end of the day man is to be delivered, not only from every form of economic exploitation but also from all the major evils of society, these years of dictatorship and the suffering of "class enemies" are to the Communist a small price to pay for so great a good.

One extenuating factor is often present where we find evidences of Communist terror—the terror is a stage in a vicious circle in which some kind of reactionary terror has preceded. In eastern Europe, in Yugoslavia for example, there seems to be little to choose between red and white forms of terror. Martin Ebon says in his survey of Communism in the Balkans that "those nations which suppressed Communism most ruthlessly in the past today have the most dictatorial Communist governments."[27] Communism first came to power in a nation that had had no experience of political freedom and that had provided many examples of ruthless treatment of political oppo-

---

[27] Martin Ebon, *World Communism Today* (New York: Whittlesey House, 1948), p. 113.

nents. The Communists were able to follow these examples with an efficiency unknown to the Czarist regime, and the pattern of Communist methods continues to be developed in nations which have long been on the edge of anarchy and civil war, and which have never had the conditions that encourage attitudes of political tolerance.

We can only speculate as to whether or not Communism would have developed a more moderate type of regime and more tolerant attitudes if it had gained power first in a nation that had had long experience of political and personal freedom. That is a different question from the question as to whether Communism will be more moderate now if exported to such a country. There is less chance of that because the stamp has been put upon Communism by the Russian experience, and many of the leaders of Western Communist movements have had their period of apprenticeship in Russia. Not only is there the Russian background of despotism and the absence in Russia of the results of a successful liberal political revolution, there is also the curious compound of the faith in the messianic role of the proletariat with the faith in the messianic role of Russia that has had a long history in Russian culture. This adds a quality to Russian Communism that is peculiarly difficult for Americans and western Europeans to understand. As Berdyaev once said: "Something has happened which Marx and the western Marxists could not have foreseen, and that is a sort of identification of two messianisms, the messianism of the Russian people and the messianism of the proletariat."[28] It is significant that Berdyaev himself, especially in his book *The Russian Idea*, exemplifies this

---

[28] *Origin of Russian Communism*, p. 173.

same Russian messianism and makes claims for the role of the Russian people that sound fantastic to all non-Russian readers. I shall not attempt to speculate on the degree to which this merging of these two claims for the special redemptive role of a particular group, in the one case a class and in the other case a nation, has increased the fanaticism and hence the ruthlessness of the Communist movement with which we have to deal. I emphasize this problem because Western critics of Communism should keep their minds open to the distinctively Russian sources of its authoritarianism, its hospitality to despotism in the state, and its ruthless fanaticism.

It would be a satisfaction if it were possible to consider the good and evil in Communism and come to the conclusion that there is enough good in it to become an antidote to the evil. But the situation seems to be that there is nothing about present economic reforms or about the promises for the future that dulls the edge of Communist terror and Communist tyranny when once Communists come to control the state machinery. Their idealistic promises become an excuse for the terror and the tyranny. The very fact that their teaching assumes an automatic withering away of the state prevents any realistic dealing with the problem of freedom, even in the case of those Communists who care most about it. Meanwhile the tendency of dictatorship to perpetuate itself is the dominant fact, and it is difficult to foresee any future escape from it. Hesitation to relinquish power by those who have enjoyed it, fear that those who have been victims of terror will avenge themselves when once power is shared—these are the most obvious difficulties. But deeper and more pervasive than either is the fact that the institutions of political and personal freedom require moral and spiritual preparation that Communism does nothing to provide. They can be lost in a reckless moment but they can be established only when a people has a rare combination of political skill and loyalty to the values that freedom makes possible in personal life.

3

The Significance of Develop-
ments in Russia Since Stalin

WHAT CAN BE SAID about developments in Russia since
the death of Stalin? Are there any generalizations which
can be made with confidence; if so, do they have any
bearing on our attitude toward Communism?

Efforts to answer these questions must be cautious
and tentative. It is difficult to know whose testimony
to take most seriously, whether we are thinking of jour-
nalists, distinguished travelers who have their hours with
Khrushchev, or academic experts on Russia. Since I
belong to none of those categories, I have to give some
general impressions which are based on the effort to
learn from all three types of testimony. There are some
facts which are so well known that they do not require
any special testimony, for example, the fact that Russia
was the first to hit the moon and the fact that Khrushchev's defeated rivals are still alive.

The strongest impression I have received from all
that we have learned about Russia in the past few years
is that the Communist system has been astonishingly
successful on its own terms. The idea that has been

Note the explanation in the Preface of the relation between this
chapter and the preceding one.

widely held in this country that because Communism denies what we regard as precious forms of freedom, it must necessarily defeat itself, and that if we keep up the pressure against it long enough, it will fold up because of the evil in it, is plainly false. Sputnik became a symbol of the strength of the Communist system. Russian education, however it may be criticized for particular methods or for the neglect of particular content, is an amazing demonstration of economic, intellectual, and administrative effectiveness. Soviet production increases sensationally, and after decades of deprivation the Russians as consumers are beginning to benefit from it. The welfare services, especially the provision for medical care, have at last drawn grudging admiration from critics. In science, technology, production, and in such indices of welfare as the increase of life expectancy, Communism in Russia has been successful. Its success has increased support for the system, whether or not this means belief in the ideology, in Russia; and it has become a major source of attraction among peoples that need in as short a time as possible a social and a technological revolution.

The second most important impression which I receive is that the Russian people are no longer so afraid of their government as they were under Stalin. Many political prisoners have been released. The secret police are less pervasive. There is less fear of being seen with foreigners, even with Americans. In general there has been a notable relaxation of the terror, so that the ordinary citizen is not afraid of disappearing into a prison or concentration camp and the factory manager is less afraid that any mistake will be treated as a crime to which a severe punishment is attached.

There remains uncertainty as to how far this trend has gone and as to how secure it is. Some good observers claim that the prisons and labor camps have been almost emptied of political prisoners. Sir William Hayter, who was the British Ambassador in Moscow from 1953-57, says outright that Khrushchev has stopped sudden arrests and has emptied the cencentration camps.[1] John Gunther said as early as 1957: "The labor camps, as of today, have been largely done away with for political prisoners."[2] Governor Averill Harriman on the basis of a short visit to Russia made the same claim. His previous experience as Ambassador to Russia and his early insight into the evils of Stalinism give some weight to his observations.

Harrison Salisbury, in his remarkable series of articles in the *New York Times* in September, 1959, emphasizes the end of the forced labor camps as penal institutions for political prisoners. He makes this general comment about the reduction of the political terror: "It may be that Georgi A. Zhukov, chairman of the Soviet States Committee on Cultural Relations, is exaggerating when he says that there is no longer a single political prisoner in the Soviet Union. But he is not exaggerating much."[3]

In a recent and certainly very cautious academic study of conditions in Russia, *The Soviet Citizen*,[4] one of the Harvard studies of Soviet Russia based upon intensive interviewing of exiles from Russia and on some contemporary observation, the authors say that the terror is "vastly reduced." (p. 393) They speak of "the release of thousands from forced labor camps," of "the tremendous reduction of political arrests to the point

---

[1] *The Observer*, London, August 16, 1959.

[2] John Gunther, *Inside Russia Today* (New York: Harper & Brothers, 1957), p. 234.

[3] *New York Times*, September 10, 1959.

[4] Alex Inkeles and Raymond A. Bauer, *The Soviet Citizen* (Cambridge: Harvard University Press, 1959).

where they affect only a small proportion of the population." (p. 378) Again they say that "the terror is not likely to be applied again on a mass scale, at least not at home." (p. 396) They assume that one major reason for the reduction of the terror is that most Russians are reasonably satisfied with the main outlines of the system and that there is enough spontaneous conformity to make the harsher methods of securing conformity unnecessary.

Dr. Philip E. Mosely, one of the most careful students of the Soviet Union, who does not often make very optimistic statements about it, goes quite far in stressing the real changes for the better that have taken place for the average citizen. He writes as follows:

> Today, factory managers, collective farm chairmen, artists and writers, Party officials of many ranks no longer fear sudden disappearance, whether through imprisonment or execution or exile to labor camps or to forced residence. To a great extent the atmosphere of terror has been lifted.

He gives a very cautious judgment about the judicial system, indicating that the control by the Party apparatus remains, and yet he is able to say that "some important improvements have been made in the administration of justice. To a considerable extent the reforms of the past two years have separated the functions of investigation, prosecution, and trial." After citing the defects that remain in a system that is still in the main totalitarian, he says: "Still, with all these defects, intolerable in a true system of law, the new conditions of justice offer a vast improvement over those of Stalin's days, especially for non-political offenders."[5]

George Kennan, who knows Russia so well, has sum-

---

[5] *Foreign Affairs,* April 1961, pp. 345-346.

marized the new situation in a recent address. He said that "what we now see in the Soviet Union represents a compromise," that it has "gone so far as to represent a highly significant departure from Stalinism and an essential alteration of the nature of the regime." He said: "A younger generation is growing up which is habituated to a greater freedom and to greater expectations of personal comfort than they could have dreamed of some years back. It would be extremely difficult today to turn the clock back."[6]

It is an open question as to how far during this period of relaxation institutions may develop which provide a more reliable protection of individual rights. So far this has not taken place, and until it does take place some of these gains will remain precarious. The Russians have, at least, during this period condemned the lawless methods of conducting trials under Stalin, and a good deal has been thought and said about improving the legal system in order to reduce arbitrariness. It is hardly fair to expect Russia to establish the best Anglo-Saxon institutions of justice in a few decades.

There are three other aspects of the present situation which may be less clear than these two general impressions but need to be kept in mind as we try to estimate the significance of what is happening in Russia.

1. The first is the broadening of the political base of the dictatorship. Khrushchev is the unchallenged head of the government and he has reached his present position of power by means of the most astute and daring maneuvers. But he did this by appealing from the small Presidium to the much larger Central Committee which

---

[6] Quoted in a Paris dispatch, *New York Post*, October 6, 1959.

supported him against his rivals. Reinhold Niebuhr has been impressed by this appeal to the larger group as involving an analogy to the early stages of the development of more broadly based political institutions in England. He says that there is evidently "something like a Whig aristocracy in the Russian system of the Central Committee." He adds: "Clearly there is a possibility of historical development within this system, though one must not paint the prospects in too bright colors."[7] The fact that Khrushchev does not imprison or execute his rivals indicates that within the Kremlin there is an atmosphere less poisoned by fear than under Stalin. Edward Crankshaw notes that Khrushchev's power depends upon acceptance of it by his present colleagues, that he and they know this, and that, as a result, they fear him less and he is less arbitrary with them than was true of relationships within Stalin's Kremlin.[8] Russia is still run by an oligarchy and a tiny one at that; it is still a dictatorship that is controlled by a few leaders of the party. But one-man rule is gone and there also seems to be some responsiveness to public opinion in such matters as the desire of the people for consumers' goods and, perhaps, to the desire of the people for peace. The fact that public opinion cannot express itself through free elections does not mean that it has no power to influence the decisions of an oligarchy that is wise enough to keep its ear to the ground.

These political developments are minimal and they may have little to do with the development of democratic political institutions. Also, as Reinhold Niebuhr points out, there are in the Russian nation no great inde-

---

[7] Reinhold Niebuhr, *The Structure of Nations and Empires* (New York: Charles Scribner's Sons, 1959), p. 283.

[8] *Atlantic Monthly*, May, 1959, p. 29.

pendent sources of power to resist the political power of
the oligarchy. He says that in the development of liberty
in democratic countries both "property" and "conscience" were such sources of power.[9] It remains true
that the political rulers are guardians of the ideology
which is the guide of conscience for those who are still
believers. How far other guides of conscience may
arise as the ideology loses hold on the minds of people
remains to be seen.

2. The second change is the passing of the revolutionary generation with its fanatical belief in the Marxist-Leninist ideology. Stalin set himself up as an in-
terpreter of the official doctrine and claimed for his
teaching the authority of the master. Today the Marxist-
Leninist symbols and concepts remain the chief furniture
of the mind in Russia. This ideology still sets intellectual
limits and still provides the lens through which most
Russians view the outside world. Certainly there is not
likely to be in the foreseeable future a repudiation of the
Marxist-Leninist philosophy or of the ultimate Communist goals which are involved in it. As I shall emphasize later, the blind spot on religion of both Marx and
Lenin, which became a part of the official Communist
teaching, will long be a factor in preventing a large
part of the Russian population, especially the "progressive" and sophisticated people, from being open to the
truth of the gospel.

While all of these things may be true and, in so far
as they are true, they are tragic, it may also be true
that the Russians of the younger generation are less convinced about the basic philosophy and less preoccupied
with Communisim's ultimate goals. Pride in national

---

[9] *The Structure of Nations and Empires,* p. 285.

achievements may arouse more emotion than loyalty to the cause of world revolution. The quite extraordinary fact that the Russian people, subjected to decades of propaganda about the outside world and especially about the United States, are spontaneously friendly to Americans indicates that this indoctrination has not produced single-track, dehumanized puppets. The educational system with its great emphasis on science and technology may not of itself produce people who are politically critical any more than education in Germany prevented Hitlerism, but it is more likely to produce builders and people concerned about solving the concrete problems of their own national society than revolutionaries and fanatical ideologues. As one student of Russian affairs has said, many of the products of the Russian educational system have a primary concern for professional competence. They may still live in the intellectual world of Marxist symbols and concepts because they have never been exposed to any other, but while these are taken for granted, they do not control the whole mind but are combined with a "deeply felt urge to acquire autonomy in one's professional role and in a sector of private life."[10] This illuminating study of Soviet intellectuals indicates that Soviet education has not produced a generation possessed by the total Communist world view, but rather, while that world view is there, the real concern is for "more modest, more personal and perhaps more human values."[11]

If these observations are true about some of the results of Russian education, and perhaps even more the results of the passing of the generations and of new

---

[10] Leopold H. Haimson, "Three Generations of the Soviet Intelligentsia," *Foreign Affairs*, January, 1959, p. 244.

[11] *Ibid.*

historical experiences, they may mean, first, that the ideological drive to remake the world with or without its consent according to the Communist pattern will lose momentum. This may have an enormous practical effect if it causes the Russians to have more limited goals in the international sphere. A crusading nation with vast power is a menace to its neighbors, but when the crusade loses incentive even if there is no formal renunciation of its goals, adjustments on a live-and-let-live basis may be possible. The deepest suspicion of Russian pleas for peaceful co-existence are based upon the fear that the Russians are only playing for time and softening up the opposition with the ultimate objective of imposing their system on the world. It is possible that with each decade the motive to impose their system on others will lose strength.

A second consequence of these intellectual changes is that they will set limits to the extension of totalitarian control over the culture. Accommodation to political authority in most things may remain, but if, as in Stalin's time, the political authorities begin again to set themselves up as the ultimate authorities in all matters—even science, music, art, and language—they will meet with considerable resistance. It is an encouraging sign that, according to Harrison Salisbury, Khrushchev regrets the Pasternak affair and "is deeply committed to greater cultural freedoms."[12]

Salisbury noted on a trip through the Soviet Union in late 1961 a surprising amount of open discussion of public affairs. He writes that, while there are still limits to debate, "it is evident to anyone who has seen much of the Soviet Union over recent years that there is more free

---

[12] *New York Times*, September 14, 1959.

talk and criticism at almost every level of society since Stalin launched his first purges in late 1934 and early 1935." He adds: "It is also evident that this kind of relaxation in comment, criticism, and ordinary conversation is being deliberately and consciously encouraged by Mr. Khrushchev and his closest associates."[13]

It is one of the great spiritual tragedies of our time that the narrow philosophy of dialectical materialism and the deep prejudice against religion are so thoroughly imbedded in the Communist world view. Freedom for philosophical thought and full freedom to propagate religion may come late. Yet even here, the degree of preoccupation with official dogmas may change enough to allow more freedom than is officially recognized. The Church is accorded considerable freedom within its own walls. Legal barriers to public teaching of religion and cultural obstacles to its reception remain, but a church that makes the most of freedom within its own life will preserve a Christian culture within a Marxist culture and no one can say how much the power of the gospel can make itself felt even when the external obstacles are great. The entrance of the Russian Orthodox Church and other Orthodox churches from Communist countries into the World Council of Churches at least involves for them greater freedom of contact with the outside world. It is an essential form of religious freedom to be able to have relationships with the larger Church beyond the nation.

3. A third long-term change seems to be in process: the emphasis by the Russian people themselves on the improvement of their living standards, the increase of consumers' goods. The more they become involved in the

---

13 *New York Times*, January 7, 1962.

same interests and pursuits as those which occupy people in the so-called bourgeois countries, the less they are likely to be governed by a revolutionary ideology. A better standard of living for the average family in Russia is likely to shift interest from the utopian future seen through the lens of ideology to the concretely improving present. I do not want to overemphasize this point by itself. A reversal of the present trend toward political moderation and the return of the ruthless tyranny of the party oligarchy might make possible once again the manipulation of the people for Communist ends that are incompatible with their obvious interests. The habit of political passivity even where there is little or no ideological conviction would be favorable to such a reversal. But will there be a strong enough motive at the center to impose such a reversal on the nation? The reversal itself would be more difficult to achieve than the maintenance of the ruthless tyranny before the reforms after Stalin's death. All that we can say here is that historical gains are not secure and that catastrophic forms of retrogression are possible in most, if not all, situations.

Suppose that the relatively optimistic interpretation of changes in Russia which I have given is correct, how should it affect our attitude toward Communism? Should Christians become less opposed to Communism as an alternative for nations which do need revolutionary changes? Should we let down our guard where Communism is a conspiracy or a revolutionary force within a non-Communist country? Should we minimize the deep conflicts between Christian faith and the Communist ideology?

I think that these changes in Russia should alter our attitude to Communism in one respect but that in most contexts the answer to those questions should be "no."

We should now take a much more positive attitude toward Russia as a Communist nation. Russia has paid the price and after forty years of great suffering is coming out on the other side with gains that we should respect. Certainly the idea of trying to overcome Communism in Russia is an absurdity long since renounced by all who are responsible for American policy. But there remains a fanatical form of anti-Communism that insists on reading all developments negatively in ideological terms. This kind of anti-Communism blinds many people to realities. We should today take a more positive attitude toward many of the institutions of Soviet Russia and regard them as part of a massive human experiment that should be allowed to have its chance without hostility on our part.

We can expect a future of competition between this experiment and all of the rival systems, semi-socialist or semi-capitalist, which emphasize political and cultural and spiritual freedom. That competition should not prevent interaction between the systems, and it may be possible in the future for Americans to admit that in some matters of economic organization, and especially in provision for social services, they can learn something from the Russians! Already there is an undercurrent of such an admission in the numerous American studies of Russian education. Mutual respect between the two countries requires something from us as well as from the Russians, and this something may be our capacity to view Russian institutions concretely with less distortion on our part by a relentless anti-Communism.

So much for the positive effect of the changes in Russia. This, however, should not obscure the following considerations which ought still to control our attitude toward Communism and its spread in the world.

1. Even though Russian institutions may be better than appeared possible during the period of Stalinism, Stanlinism was no accident. It did involve some paranoiac excesses that were accidental, but in the main the ruthlessness was determined by the ends sought—by the task of transforming an economically backward nation into an advanced industrialized nation in a few decades. The tyranny was the means of national discipline that made possible so costly an effort for the sake of rewards which only a future generation would enjoy. The terrible evils of Stalinism were at least in large part the price paid for Russian capacity to survive the war and for some of the achievements of the Soviet system today. The absolutism of Communism, and the way in which its utopian hope provides rationalizations for cruel short cuts to the establishment of the power of the party, remains important. Even though the present stage in Russia may suggest that this absolutism and these rationalizations lose strength, we never know how much any new Communist experiment may be controlled by them.

It is possible that in another country Communism may prove to be more moderate in the formative period, but any nation that chooses Communism is taking a grave risk of having to endure what Russia has endured. China is in the early stages of Communism. She is going through a similar period of a tyrannical discipline, and the pressure of the ideology upon the minds of the people seems to be equal to, if not greater than, anything known in Russia. In fact, the invasion of private life seems to be greater in China than in Russia. The vast Chinese population may have produced even more disregard of the individual life than in Russia. Mao Tsetung has not been as cruel in purging his colleagues as was Stalin, but the purging of "class enemies" and the discipline of the people seems to have been no less cruel than anything of which we know in Russia. So the experience of Russia, reinforced by the experience of China, remains a terrible warning to any nation that is tempted to choose Communism.

2. The religious struggle of Christians with many aspects of Communist teaching and of the Communist way of life should continue unabated. This should not be a self-righteous holy cold war. If there are relaxations of terror and improvements in communications between Christians and Communists, the form of the struggle will be altered. It may be primarily a matter of day-by-day personal witness in love and of the impact of the regular work of the churches.

Christian witness and service in relation to Communist cultures in many ways will not differ from Christian witness and service in relation to any of our secularized industrialized societies. In Communist countries and here in the United States we face the same gods of scientism and technology and materialism. But the differences will still be important. In Communist societies the official ideology which is favored in the educational system and. in all the pressures that come from governments that control the channels of communication is atheistic and antireligious. Even if it were not for the explicit atheism, the official philosophy is a kind of naturalism contrary to the Christian understanding of God and man. In Russia the churches are given more internal freedom than was true during most of the history of Communist Russia, but still public religious witness is generally prevented and the religious education of youth is greatly curtailed. In some other Communist countries the conflict between church and state is at its peak, especially in East Germany where the Church is strong enough to be a center of spiritual opposition to the regime whose hold upon the people is known to be precarious.

The antireligious side of Communist teaching may be disguised or soft-pedaled during the early stages of Communist propaganda or penetration in a country, but Christians in all countries which are in any degree tempted by Communism should not allow themselves to forget that the opposition of Communism to religion is not peripheral. It is built into the intellectual world view of Communism and it is strengthened by the fact that Communism in practice during the height of its ideological confidence becomes a substitute for religion, and also by the fact that a Communist state would not tolerate churches which prove to be centers of criticism of its policies or of opposition to its control of the mind. A period of general relaxation may reduce the pressures on the churches, and a less wholehearted belief in the claims of the ideology may open many minds to religious truth without there having to be any explicit changes in the role of religion in the culture.

These aspects of a Communist society cause the religious problem to be quite different from what it is in a pluralistic and relatively free society, no matter how much the culture may be influenced by intellectual scientism and practical materialism. It may be true that in some situations the more explicit conflict is spiritually better for the Church than for it to be corrupted and smothered in freedom by an alien culture that does lip service to it. There is not such a degree of corruption and smothering in the United States as to constitute a liability as great as the liability that is present when the state deliberately draws the youth away from the Church and denies to it all opportunities for public teaching and witness.

3. Even if we revise our judgment about the likely developments of Communism in Russia, this should not permit us to be less opposed to the imposition of Communisim by Russia or China upon other countries. The international Communist movement is still dynamic and, especially in Asia, it remains a threat to freedom. The Russian action in Hungary in 1956 in suppressing by armed force a popular revolution, and the defense of the action by means of a typical propagandist distortion of the events in Hungary, remains a warning that even the Russia of Khrushchev can become involved in Stalinist forms of repression outside its borders. It collaborates with a shabby Stalinist tyranny in East Germany. The cold-blooded execution of Imre Nagy many months after the Hungarian revolution was a warning of what is still possible. It may be that in the case of Hungary the Russians were in a panic as they saw the danger that their whole western defense system might crumble.

The internal relationships and strategic plans within world Communism, and especially the relationship of Russia to China, give rise to much speculation. In the context of the Communist conspiracy and of the fomenting of revolution in Asian countries the nations that are still free from Communist control must still be on the alert. Russia's main drive may be to prove by example the superiority of Communism, but at hand there are these other means—conspiracy and readiness for military pressures—which can be used to extend Communism and these are likely to be used if the risks are not too great. China may be the more dynamic partner in the Communist alliance and, as I have said, it borders on the more vulnerable nations, but Russia may still at times run interference for China internationally and give many kinds of support to Communist expansion by the combination of outside pressure and internal revolt which the Russians may defend as not involving the imposing of Communism on an unwilling nation. We shall have to live for a long time with the problem posed by the imperialism of international Communism even if it should turn out that Russia is not the prime mover. More fundamental than the overt forms of direct or indirect aggression will be the attraction of Communist societies and the overwhelming social and economic problems and the weak governments in some countries. Those countries as they face their own decisions should not be allowed to forget to what a bitter political and cultural and spiritual tyranny Communism will subject their people for at least a generation.

4. There is no assurance that such a ruthless tyranny might not continue for an indeterminate period. Even now in Russia the party leaders decide how much freedom there is to be. They do not decide this in a vacuum and they are at times responsive to popular demands, but there is no structure within Communist government that can be depended on as a source of self-correction. In contrast, the great merit of democracy is that the process of self-correction is built into it. A nation without effective democratic institutions, if it has as a matter of custom a measure of cultural freedom, can be changed by an open dialogue on public issues. But it is exactly this dialogue which is lacking in a Communist society except as its leaders decide to permit it. At least this is the tendency. We should not assume that it is an irreversible tendency, but it is a stubborn one that limits the degree of confidence that we can have in the emergence of a more responsible government and a more open society.

This concern for some institutional limits upon power and safeguards for freedom and openness should not cause us to judge the Communist nations in terms of Anglo-Saxon democracy as a yardstick. Many nations in the so-called West would not do well when measured by that yardstick and both the Communist nations and many new nations, as they develop, will have to experiment with many forms of political institutions which will be different from our type of democracy. Without being less opposed to tyranny or to the efforts of totalitarian states to control the minds of men, we shall have to be tolerant of the political experiments of other nations which are more authoritarian than democracy. Threats of anarchy and the necessity of rapid but guided social changes under stress create problems which may be too much for democracy. While this must be said, no political institutions can be tolerable unless they move toward the limited state, freedom of expression, and participation by the people in government.[14]

Now I want to return, first, to my earlier emphasis on a more positive attitude toward Russia. These threats from international Communism still exist, but it is a human movement that is influenced by history as well as by ideology and the changes in Russia are an important part of that history. Communists who are engaged in building a new society are different from Communists who are engaged in conspiracy or revolution. We should ungrudgingly praise many of their achievements and we should congratulate the present rulers of Russia that they have brought their country out of the darkness of Stalinism. We must not insist that they use our slogans before we show them respect. Nor should we continue the black

---

[14] See the discussions of this problem in the Report of the Service Section of the New Delhi Assembly of the World Council of Churches (1961). *New Delhi Speaks* (New York: Association Press, 1962).

and white tendency to divide the world between slave nations and free nations. Nor should we continue to assume that their gains must be our losses. And always the more personal and cultural interchange there is between our people and theirs, the better.[15]

Secondly, I want to re-emphasize my earlier comments on the diversity within the Communist world. Already there is a fierce ideological conflict between the Soviet Union and its anti-Stalinist partners on one side and China and Albania on the other. This kind of conflict may result in what Professor Brzezinski calls "a gradual relativization of the formerly absolutist ideology."[16] Also the combination of Communism with a national spirit as different as the spirit of Poland from the spirit of Russia has produced a somewhat liberalized Communism that is consistent with much intellectual freedom. When we become more accustomed to this fact of diversity within the Communist world, we shall be less inclined to regard Communism as one vast monolithic embodiment of evil.

---

[15] Professor William Ernest Hocking's book *The Strength of Men and Nations,* Harper, 1959, bravely projects a way of thinking about the essential humanity of the Communists which is a relief after years of the mentality of the cold war. It is good to read the following sentence: "Whatever the mystery of Soviet motivation, however alien the Slavonic temperament and capacity for wile may be felt to be, there can be no shadow of doubt that they who share with us an official willingness to prepare weapons for the collective extinction of populations entertain not alone a fear of retaliation but an inward revulsion to their use." (p. 188) It is significant that it is now possible to make such assertions.

[16] *Foreign Affairs,* April, 1961, p. 442.

4

The Main Issues Between Christianity and Communism

IT HAS often been pointed out that Communism could only have been developed on soil prepared by Christianity. Its emphasis upon the significance of what happens in human history is itself a reflection of the biblical view of history as the arena of God's activity. The acceptance of the importance of human history, of the collective decisions of men, of time and events and nations, is so much taken for granted among us that it is easy to forget that it represents a quite distinctive view of life not characteristic of classical antiquity or of contemporary cultures uninfluenced by the Judaeo-Christian tradition. There is, therefore, in Communism a deposit of Christian influence of great importance, in contrast, for example, with Neoplatonism or Buddhism, and with other religious systems characterized by the effort to escape from time and history to the changeless and the eternal.

Also, Communism inherits from the biblical faith its passion for social justice. As Paul Tillich says: "Both prophetism [the faith of the Old Testament prophets] and Marxism regard the fight between good and evil forces as the main content of history, describing the evil forces as mainly the forces of injustice and envisaging the ultimate triumph of justice."[1] The Christian hope for the kingdom of God has often been compared and contrasted with the Communist hope for the new order that will ultimately be established after the complete triumph of the revolution. The differences are great, since Communism identifies its goal with a new society that it expects to be fully established in the course of history; whereas Christians, while they may differ on the extent to which the kingdom will be approximated in any social order, have usually regarded the kingdom of God as the source of judgment upon every social order. One can discern in Communism a distortion of real elements in the Judaeo-Christian tradition. This is why Jacques Maritain, the late Archbishop William Temple, and other Christian thinkers have spoken of Communism as "a Christian heresy" in order to distinguish it from a totally pagan movement such as National Socialism.

We can go further and say that Communism, as is often the case with heresy, is a response to a certain one-sidedness in the development of the Christianity of the churches; and it is a corrective that all Christians must take seriously. I have already mentioned this but now I want to emphasize it. Communism has acted as a reminder of the responsibility of Christians and of the Church to seek the realization of more equal justice in society. Its bitter attacks upon conventional religion have had a measure of justification because of the excessive individualism of evangelical Protestantism and because of the identification of Protestant churches with the middle classes and of both Roman and Orthodox churches with the established political and social orders

---

[1] Paul Tillich, *The Protestant Era* (Chicago: University of Chicago Press, 1948), p. 254.

of the various countries in which they have been dominant.

It is one of the most fateful facts in modern European
history that during the nineteenth century when our industrial society was taking shape, the working classes of
most countries came to believe sincerely that the
churches were against them. This stereotype of religion
in the minds of the working classes, especially of Communists and Social Democrats, has persisted until now.
A great change has come in the teachings and attitudes
of the churches within the past half century, but it can
hardly be denied that this change was in large part a
result of the pressure from the radical movements that
found their stimulus in Marxism. It has become commonplace among Protestants to say these things. The
bitter propaganda against Communism by Roman
Catholics often has a self-righteous quality which is the
result of the failure of official Roman Catholicism to
admit the degree of the Church's own responsibility for
the antireligious character of Communism. Jacques
Maritain, the Catholic philosopher who speaks for himself and not for the Church, is able to do full justice to
the responsibility of Christians for the aspects of Communism that they must oppose. He asks: "What is the
cause of this [the atheism of Communism]?" He answers:
"It is, I hold, because it originates, chiefly through the
fault of a Christian world unfaithful to its own principles,
in a profound sense of resentment, not only against the
Christian world, but—and here lies the tragedy—against
Christianity itself."[2]

Nicolas Berdyaev, himself an exiled victim of the anti-

---

[2] Jacques Maritain, *True Humanism* (New York: Charles Scribner's Sons, 1938), p. 33.

Christian teaching and policy of Russian Communism, has said the same thing continually. In one place he says: "Christians, who condemn the Communists for their godlessness and antireligious persecutions, cannot lay the whole blame solely upon these godless Communists; they must assign part of the blame to themselves, and that a considerable part. They must be not only accusers and judges; they must also be penitents. Have Christians done very much for the realization of Christian justice in social life? Have they striven to realize the brotherhood of man without that hatred and violence of which they accuse the Communists? The sins of Christians, the sins of historical churches, have been very great, and these sins bring with them their just punishment."[3]

It is one of the difficulties in finding the right way of dealing with Communism that, without in any way nullifying what has been said in the last paragraphs, we must not suppose that it alters the objective fact that at essential points Christianity and Communism are in profound conflict. A recognition of the truth in what has been said should affect the spirit in which Christians oppose Communism; above all, it should help us to realize that humanity needs to be delivered both from Communism and from a one-sided form of Christianity.

There is one obvious difference between Christianity and all other religions and all other systems of life and thought: it comes from the fact that Christianity affirms belief in a particular revelation and in particular redemptive acts of God in history. The faith that Christ was the center of a series of historical events in which God has sought to draw men to himself is so distinctive that it

---

[3] *Origin of Russian Communism*, pp. 207, 208.

separates Christianity not only from Communism but from all non-Christian religions and philosophies.

Though this faith is quite foreign to Communism and would indeed be rejected as obscurantist nonsense by Communist thinkers who believe that science interpreted by Marxist philosophy is the beginning and end of human wisdom, it may throw some light on the nature of both Christianity and Communism to suggest that Communism also has its center of history which corresponds to the coming of Christ. That center is the Russian Revolution. The face of the world was changed by that event for the Communist, not in the same way but in a comparable degree to the changing of the face of the world for the Christian by the life and death and resurrection of Christ. In both cases we are dealing with faith rather than with science.

In the remainder of this chapter I shall deal with three of the most decisive points of conflict between Christianity and Communism. I have chosen to emphasize those conflicts that appear in the way in which both Christianity and Communism are related to the same problems of our historical situation. In the next chapter I shall discuss more fully the context of Christian faith within which the relation between Christianity and Communism can be more adequately understood.

Communist Atheistic Absolutism

The first and most fundamental of these conflicts may be seen in the fact that Communism absolutizes a particular movement in history and promises that this movement will bring redemption from all social evil. It teaches that there is no God above this movement and it has no understanding of the persistence of human sin—that is, of the corrupting effect of pride and self-centeredness and the will to power—within it. The great fault of Communism is not its theoretical atheism but what we may call its practical idolatry. In using the word "idolatry," I am not throwing a smear word at Communism, for the word can be quite carefully defined as the tendency to make absolute, to put in the place of God, any human or finite reality. Atheism as a theory might be sloughed off, but in this case it is a rationalization of the idolatry. I have emphasized the conviction that the false view of God that Christians have often given to the world, when they have acted as though he were a sanction for the *status quo*, is partly responsible for this error of Communism; but that in no way detracts from the tragic consequences of the error.

This belief in Communism as an absolute movement of redemption in history, in the Communist society as a substitute for God, is not only false from the Christian point of view and incompatible with the Christian's understanding of man's dependence upon God; it has at least two other consequences that should be emphasized. One is that it precludes a transcendent judgment upon every society. A nation or a social order that acknowledges that it stands under God is open to criticism and correction and growth. This is the more true when individual members of society acknowledge their personal responsibility to God as having priority over the claim of every political authority. Such individuals can bring to their society a word that may differ from the will of the majority and from the judgments of those who represent the state. If there is a church within that society which in a collective way testifies to the will of God, and if that church is not itself under the domination of the state, this openness to criticism and correction and growth will be greatly aided. In such a society personal freedom,

freedom of conscience, of thought, of expression, will have the best chance to develop and survive. All of this is dependent upon the faith held by society and its individual members in God who is above all the powers of the world.

The second consequence of this belief in Communism as an absolute movement of redemption is that it creates a false optimism that leaves people unprepared for the new forms of evil that will appear in a Communist society. I have already, in discussing the Communist view of the withering away of the state as an instrument of compulsion, referred to this optimism. The lack of a critical attitude toward the new Communist power is evident today, and we have the strange spectacle of an idealism that promises a world that will need no police but is unable to keep its own excessive use of the police under criticism. To concentrate on the capitalistic form of property as the one root of all social evil is to neglect other roots that are universally human and that will outlast capitalism and all other social systems.

This false optimism, which is based upon so simple a diagnosis of the human problem, causes those who share it to divide the world between themselves and their opponents, to claim for themselves absolute righteousness, and almost to excommunicate their opponents from the human race. This is a common tendency—this dividing of the world between one's own group and one's opponents as though the difference were one of black and white—and Christians have often shown it. But Christians are without excuse when they do it, for they should know that the very tendency to do it is a mark of the sin of pride about which they should have learned. They should know that the most significant line is not to be drawn between themselves and their opponents but rather right down through their own souls. They should know that as they stand under God—their God and the God of their opponents as well—it is only fitting to begin by confessing their own weakness and sin.

Reinhold Niebuhr, who often stresses this utopianism of Communism as its most destructive error, points out that it is an exaggerated form of the tendency in modern culture to find simple diagnoses and solutions of the human problem, to ignore the permanent roots of evil in human life, and to be unprepared for the abuse of power in the interests of a limited group in every society. He says:

> Communism turns the soft utopianism of modern culture into a hard and truculent utopianism. The difference between a soft and hard utopianism is that the former dreams of achieving an ideal society of uncoerced justice through the historical development of altruistic as against egoistic purposes; while the latter claims to embody a social system in which this miracle has already taken place. A soft utopianism projects its ideal of a perfect accord between men and nations into the future. It is therefore free of the fanaticism and truculence of the hard utopian who claims to possess the ideal society and therefore also has the right to deal ruthlessly with all enemies and opponents of his ideal.[4]

Those words may be criticized on the ground that they emphasize too much the contrast between present and future, for Communists also know that the goal lies ahead of them. Insufficient allowance may be made for the accidental historical circumstances which have helped to make Communism more ruthless than liberal schemes for achieving an ideal order. I quote them because they em-

---

[4] *Christianity and Crisis,* February 2, 1948.

phasize the kinship in origin between all programs for a complete overcoming of evil in society; and because they indicate the close relation between the fanaticism engendered by the confidence that one has the absolute solution and the ruthless tactics by which one seeks to have all obstacles to its realization removed.

Methods of Dealing with Opponents

The second area of conflict between Christianity and Communism is in regard to methods in dealing with opponents. Here we have the difficult problem of the ethic of means and the relation of means to ends. I have already said enough about the way in which Communists deal with their opponents and about the human consequences of Communist terror. There is no question about the Communist acceptance of any means that will serve the revolution. The way in which this is defended has been stated most persuasively by Arthur Koestler in his *Darkness at Noon*. Koestler is an ex-Communist who is now one of Communism's most bitter opponents, but the logic that he puts into the mouth of one of his characters states as well as it can be stated the position of those who sincerely believe that if the end is good enough it justifies any necessary means. In Koestler's novel, Ivanov, the police investigator, is arguing with an old Communist who was beginning to have his moral scruples concerning the methods that he had been forced to use by the party. In the course of the argument Ivanov says the following:

Every year several million people are killed quite pointlessly by epidemics and other natural catastrophies. And we should shrink from sacrificing a few hundred thousand for the most promising experiment in history? Not to mention the legions of those who die of undernourishment and tuberculosis in coal and quicksilver mines, rice fields, and cotton plantations. No one takes any notice of them; nobody asks why or what for; but if we shoot a few thousand objectively harmful people, the humanitarians all over the world foam at the mouth. Yes, we liquidated the parasitic part of the peasantry and let it die of starvation. It was a surgical operation which had to be done once and for all; but in the good old days before the Revolution just as many died in any dry year—only senselessly and pointlessly.[5]

We must assume that it is honestly believed that Communism is the greatest experiment in history, an experiment that is expected to rid the world of all forms of exploitation, indeed of all forms of social evil. Does not a ruthless policy, which is by hypothesis essential to realize that goal, have moral justification? Does not the very directness and quickness of the process, if indeed it is direct and quick, make it relatively less painful than the long-drawn-out suffering of the victims of existing institutions? What can Christians say in answer to these questions?

If we are to answer these questions fairly from a Christian point of view, we must deal first of all with two problems in the record of Christians themselves and see what bearing they have on the answer. The first problem is suggested by the record of religious persecution in Christian history. The second problem is suggested by Christian behavior in time of war and in such situations as those created by the resistance movement against the Nazis in Europe in recent years.

What difference is there between Communist terror and religious persecution that has been carried on by both Catholics and Protestants in the past? Theoretically I can see some difference when one of the motives behind a

---

[5] Arthur Koestler, *Darkness at Noon*, Penguin Signet Edition, pp. 116–117.

policy of persecution is a misguided and desperate attempt to save the souls of the persecuted. Here the opponent is not merely an obstacle to be removed but a person to be redeemed *for his own sake*. How often this motive was a real factor in religious persecution I cannot say, but it did reconcile many sensitive Christians to a practice which must have been repellent. But where religious persecution has been controlled chiefly by the desire to preserve religious uniformity in the nation, it has involved the same subordination of human souls to a political purpose that is characteristic of Communism. It is significant that one can see in the legend of the Grand Inquisitor in Dostoevsky's *The Brothers Karamazov* (which is one of the greatest appeals for spiritual freedom ever written) an attack both on the Church for its policies of regimentation and persecution and on the precursors of Russian Communism in whom Dostoevsky discerned the willingness to subordinate the freedom of the soul to a political program. So far as the history of Christian behavior is concerned, there has been in the past no clear case in principle against Communist methods. Today religious persecution has been totally abandoned by Protestant Christianity as a method of dealing with opponents. Roman Catholicism, in some countries where it is the dominant Church, still acts on the principle that the state should practice discrimination in the interests of the true Church, but it has abandoned the more cruel forms of persecution.[6]

If we move from a consideration of what Christians have done, and still may do, in some situations to a con-

---

[6] This whole matter of the use of political power in the interests of the Roman Catholic Church to hinder the expression of "error" by other religious bodies in a Catholic state is now very much in debate in principle among Roman Catholic thinkers. There is an im-

sideration of what they should do if they understand the meaning of their own faith, one can speak decisively. To use external pressure on any person to convert him even for his own sake is to tempt him to be insincere; it is a practice that is based upon a complete miscalculation concerning the way in which the human spirit comes to respond to religious truth. Most religious persecution has also been based upon an arrogant assumption not only of the absoluteness of the truth to which one's own doctrines point but even of the absoluteness of one's own formulation of doctrine or of one's own religious institutions. The very process increases the hardness and arrogance of the persecutor. The kind of religious persecution that is designed to protect society from error or to preserve the religious unity of the nation is a much deeper offense against Christian love. It sacrifices persons to a religious policy. It sins against their consciences and corrupts the religious life of the community and destroys the meaning of truth, for it makes power the arbiter of truth. This is the only kind of persecution that bears any resemblance in principle to Communist terror, and both should be condemned for the same reasons. This is one area in which there has been a real growth in the Christian mind during the modern period. Today Christian assumptions on the ethics of persecution are surely more in harmony with the New Testament teaching that comes to us from a period before Christians were tempted to use political power to coerce the souls of others. The ages of religious persecution may have been ages of faith but they often needed to hear the words: "And if

portant trend among Roman Catholics which would defend the religious liberty of religious minorities in "error" even in a nation in which the Roman Church can influence the state through a large Roman Catholic majority.

I have all faith, so as to remove mountains, but have not love, I am nothing."

Far more serious is the problem raised by the behavior of Christians in war or in situations in which they have resisted oppression by conspiracy, as in the case of the European resistance against National Socialism, a type of resistance that is being repeated today in some countries by those who must face the Communist terror.

The actual behavior of Christians and of nations which acknowledge Christian standards has been much less different from that of Communists than they suppose. In the recent war, most Christian statesmen and most Christian citizens have acted on the assumption that anything—or almost anything—was permissible if it was believed to be necessary to victory. Here I am not speaking of what Christians should think or do but I am comparing the actual behavior of Christians with that of Communists, which is only fair. There have been some criticisms in the churches of various methods that were used in the recent war, but it would be difficult to maintain that among most of the members of the American churches there was a clear witness against such horrors as obliteration bombing, which in some cases bombed or burned to death as many as two hundred thousand persons in a single night. As for the use of the atomic bomb over Hiroshima and Nagasaki, there were more protests from Christians who saw in this not only an isolated atrocity but a fateful example by America to the world for all time. But even in this case the bad conscience that was created was never very effectively expressed, and men of integrity and sensitivity, such as President Harry S. Truman and Secretary Henry L. Stimson, defended the act on the ground that it ended the war quickly and made an invasion of Japan unnecessary, thus in the end probably saving more lives than it destroyed. This is a clear case of doing exactly what Lenin and the Communists have believed in doing, of acting on the assumption that if victory in war or revolution is important enough, anything can be justified that seems necessary for victory.

The differences of behavior in this context are more psychological than moral. Nations which acknowledge Christian standards and which are influenced by liberal humanitarianism would more readily kill with bombs in a single night a hundred thousand persons whom their people have never seen and whose condition they cannot easily imagine, than they would torture individuals near at hand to cause them to betray their associates. Such torture may take place in a police court or in isolated situations in dealing with prisoners of war, but it can never be a matter of policy as it is in Communist states.

Also, in the case of war, what is done is often put in brackets and it can be assumed that life outside the brackets will be different. One characteristic of this situation in brackets is that face-to-face relations with the enemy as persons is unusual. On the other hand the Communist in his conspiracies may work for years in the same organizations with his opponents, and his relations with them may have the outward semblance of normal personal relations. To deal with persons who are in this external relationship with oneself as though they were enemies in war must constitute for Communists who are not completely toughened a psychological, if not a moral, problem that is different from that which is usually faced by Christian citizens in war. But it is only fair to realize that, from their perspective, Communists are at war with the enemies of their class or their cause and that they expect that out of the struggle will come better results than have ever been promised to Christian citizens who sought victory in war.

Remember that, so far, I have considered only the actual behavior of nations that acknowledge Christian standards and of innumerable Christian citizens. Now I shall deal with the question: What ought Christians to do? Must we say that when military action or resistance by conspiracy is most justified there is no Christian ethic that is different from the Communist ethic?

Those who are Christian pacifists can have quite easy answers to these questions. They are convinced that any form of military action involving uncontrolled violence (not necessarily police action that can be kept within limits) is so clearly a contradiction of Christian love that it must be repudiated in advance. They may also believe that they have a positive strategy that will be more effective in resisting aggression or tyranny, but this involves political calculations about which it is more difficult to be an absolutist. In any case Christian pacifists know in advance that all military weapons are forbidden. They would have greater difficulty in the case of some of the methods that are used in resistance to secret police or other agents of political oppression. Those who are perfectionists would doubtless refuse even to lie or to forge papers in order to save someone else from arrest and torture. Others might make some compromises of this sort but would draw the line at more violent tactics, such as assassination, in order to save persons from becoming victims of such political persecution.

Christians who are not absolute pacifists in principle have much greater difficulty in stating their alternative to the Communist ethic of means. As one who agrees with them I shall try to state their alternative as I see it. I should make clear at the outset that the problem arises in those situations in which, as far as one can judge, the alternatives that face any large group, such as a nation, are severely limited. They are situations in which those who do not do what may be necessary to prevent some great evil, such as aggression that brings with it political and cultural tyranny, share responsibility for that evil. If they do act to prevent it, they may in their methods be involved in compromise but any alternative that is available may be morally worse. Those who have not faced this kind of decision do not realize the depth of evil and tragedy in human life.

The advent of atomic weapons makes the argument for the renunciation of all military force that might lead to the use of such weapons very persuasive, but if those who guide the policy of nations should come to be absolutists about this before there is developed some effective form of international control of atomic weapons, they will play into the hands of any nations that are unscrupulous enough to use the threat of atomic attacks as blackmail. And even international control might involve sanctions that would raise moral problems for the absolute pacifist. We can push the argument for a kind of practical pacifism in relation to atomic war very far, but there is one step which many Christians who are fully aware of this problem cannot take: they cannot put their communities in the position of being forced to yield to overwhelming power if there is any way of avoiding this. This is all the more true in a day in which military aggression is combined with the extension of totalitarian forms of tyranny. I raise this issue here as one of principle, and not because it is my belief that atomic attacks are likely to be the method by which Russia and Communism will choose to extend their power. They have more effective methods that are better calculated to leave something more than a desert over which to rule. Atomic destruction would be an even worse preparation for the Communist utopia than the dictatorship of the proletariat.

Christians should never admit, no matter how hard pressed they may be, that the cause that can be won or lost by military weapons or conspiracy is everything. That cause may be one to which they are loyal because they believe that to serve it is the best available expression of Christian love in the circumstances, but always there are other ethical demands that they cannot forget implied in the commandment that they love their neighbors—including their enemies. They cannot wash their hands of responsibility for the welfare of the enemy or opponent, even though this creates great complications that the strategist would like to forget. The obligation to love our enemies is not abrogated by the existence of such complications. How love of enemies or of any who are opponents of the cause can be expressed I shall discuss later. Here it is essential to emphasize that the Christian must be guided by this obligation as well as by any obligation that he may have to the cause that is at stake.

Also, Christians should not allow themselves to begin the use of force in order to establish some new social program. They should reject completely the Communist tendency to assume that the promised blessings of the new order justify any means that may prepare the way for them. That is quite different from the situation that a man or a people may face when they must seek to prevent some intolerable evil from overwhelming them. What may be necessary in that case cannot be justified in some other situation by grandiose promises for the future. It can only be justified in relation to the known reality of the evil that threatens. In this case, the use of violence is a last desperate resort when the alternative, as far as one can judge, is even worse. There is a parallel to this position in the case of the current discussion of the ethics of a preventive war. Nations in the age of atomic weapons may be tempted to act on the basis that a preventive war is the best insurance against destruction. But for any group of people to take upon themselves the responsibility of beginning a preventive war would be, as Reinhold Niebuhr says, "to play God to historical destiny."[7] There are several kinds of fate that are now possibilities —all of which seem too evil to contemplate. One is universal destruction. Another is universal tyranny. But there is a third that would be even worse: to reduce all nations to the level on which they are normally prepared to lay waste the cities of neighboring countries in preventive wars.

Christians, whether or not they are absolute pacifists, must not act as though "everything is permitted," even in those desperate situations in which all alternatives seem to deny that for which they stand. I know from the discussions carried on in the churches during the recent war how difficult it is to draw the line. One of the most careful statements of this matter is to be found in the

---

[7] *Christianity and Society*, Summer, 1948, p. 7.

I have been impressed by the similarity between Professor Niebuhr's argument as a theologian on the issue of preventive wars and the argument by Hanson W. Baldwin, the military expert of the *New York Times*, who always sees the moral as well as the military aspects of any problem. Mr. Baldwin emphasizes the contradiction between a preventive war and the professed moral ideals of our nation, and then he stresses the "intangibles of history," showing that it would be wrong to make inevitable by our action what is not inevitable. Professor Niebuhr uses the intangibles of history to warn against the religious pretensions of those who "play God." For Mr. Baldwin's article see *Harper's Magazine*, July, 1948.

report of a commission appointed by the Federal Council of Churches during the second world war. This commission, of which Professor Robert Calhoun was the chairman, consisted of twenty-six of the most respected American Christian thinkers. It included many pacifists, though a majority of the members were non-pacifists. The following passage states both the dilemma and conclusions on which all could agree:

Total war is suited only for a totalitarian society, which as we have said is irreconcilable in principle with Christian faith in the sovereignty of God and the responsible freedom of man. No matter what the provocation, however great the extremity of military peril—even to the imminence of military defeat—the Church dare not approve a supposition that military expediency or necessity can ever rightfully become the supreme principle of human conduct. We are acutely aware how difficult it is to apply in practice this principle of resistance to claims for the supremacy in wartime of military demands and to the elevation of war even temporarily into a status of unconditional domination of human behavior. All of us agree that in war some practices cannot be regarded by the Church as justifiable: the killing of prisoners, of hostages, or of refugees to lessen military handicaps or to gain military advantages; the torture of prisoners or of hostages to gain military information, however vital; the massacre of civilian populations. Some of the signers of the report believe that certain other measures, such as rigorous blockades of foodstuffs essential to civilian life, and obliteration bombing of civilian areas, however repugnant to humane feelings, are still justifiable on Christian principles, if they are essential to the successful conduct of a war that is itself justified. A majority of the commission, moreover, believe that today war against the Axis powers, by all needful measures, is in fact justified. Others among us believe that the methods named are not justifiable on Christian principles, even though they are now practiced or defended by great numbers of sincere Christians and patriotic non-Christians, and even if they be essential to military victory for the United Nations. If it be true that modern war cannot be successfully waged without use of methods that cannot distinguish even roughly between combatants and non-combatants, or between perpetrators and victims, that fact seems to a minority in the commission to raise the question whether in modern war even the more scrupulous side can meet the conditions hitherto generally held by the Church to define a just war. On these specific issues, then, the commission is divided. On the basic principle that the Church cannot acquiesce in the supremacy of military considerations, even in war time, nor in the view that modern war may properly, even in the case of extreme peril to nation, Church, or culture, become total war, we are agreed.[8]

The deepest difference between Christianity and Communism in relation to the ethic of means is to be found, not in the precise line that we draw when we decide what is permitted, but rather in the kind of concern for the opponent as a person which all the disciplines and influences of Christian faith encourage and which is not encouraged by the disciplines and influences of Communism. This difference is primarily religious rather than ethical. The

---

[8] *Report of the Commission on the Relation of the Church to the War in the Light of the Christian Faith,* 1944, p. 68. In order to indicate the range of opinion on the commission and the measure of its authority I am listing the names of its members: Robert Lowry Calhoun, Edwin E. Aubrey, Roland H. Bainton, John C. Bennett, Conrad J. I. Bergendoff, B. Harvie Branscomb, Frank H. Caldwell, Angus Dun, Nels F. S. Ferre, Robert E. Fitch, Theodore M. Greene, Georgia E. Harkness, Walter M. Horton, John Knox, Umphrey Lee, John A. Mackay, Benjamin E. Mays, John T. McNeill, H. Richard Niebuhr, Reinhold Niebuhr, Wilhelm Pauck, Douglas V. Steere, Ernest Fremont Tittle, Henry P. Van Dusen, Theodore O. Wedel, Alexander C. Zabriskie.

Communist thinks not of the person whom God loves, even though he be the lost sheep, but of the future order of society that will be possible when all opponents are neutralized or destroyed. When Christians pray for enemies or opponents, they may be sentimental, but such prayer can be a demonstration of solidarity with the enemy or opponent under God that no conflict can destroy. This is made most vivid when it is realized that the enemy or opponent belongs to the Christian community, to some branch of the Church. In the recent war this awareness of the universal Church as transcending the military struggle was a spiritual reality that made a great difference to attitudes on both sides.

The question may be asked: Is this Christian attitude toward the enemy merely an inner feeling that is a source of self-deception or does it show itself in act? If it is real, it shows itself in act at every point where action is possible. When the Christian confronts enemies in person as prisoners, or as wounded, or as the population of occupied territory, or when there comes an opportunity for reconciliation after the military conflict is over, the inner attitude does become action. It did become action in the recent war and its aftermath. There is nothing comparable in Communism to this capacity to preserve on the religious level a relationship with enemies which is broken on the political level and which, because it is preserved, prepares the way for reconciliation on all levels.

I shall now give two illustrations of how this Christian relationship with opponents can be a reality. The first is from the experience of a Czech Christian who has become a supporter of the Communist regime in his country, Dr. Joseph Hromadka. He describes vividly his encounter with his Christian colleagues who rejected his political decision in the following passage:

> On the 25th of February, on *the* day of the February revolution [that is, revolution in Czechoslovakia], a group of my best friends and comrades came to see me and to tell me that they had ceased to trust my judgment and to follow my leadership. We had a long talk. It was one of the most dramatic moments of my life. Two days later, one of them, a man whom I deeply respect and love, came to see me again and said, "I am now much calmer than the day before yesterday. I still believe that there is nothing else to be done than to withdraw from public life and devote one's own energy to a deeper study of the Bible and to a more vigorous witness of our faith. Nevertheless, I am certain that both of us, you and I, are standing on the same ground of faith and theology. You may be wrong in your political judgment and in the way in which you interpret the present events, and I may be right. Or vice versa: you may be right, and I may be wrong. As long as we admit the limitation and weakness of our judgment, and as long as we bow our heads before the same ultimate tribunal, we are one despite our differences." That was approximately his pronouncement—and my mind and heart responded in the same spirit.[9]

Remember that this took place in Prague in the midst of a revolutionary conflict and that the author had taken sides with resolution as well as humility.[10]

---

[9] *Christianity and Crisis,* May 24, 1948.

[10] Professor Hromadka's career as an apologist for Communist regimes is now so well known that I feel I must explain my own retention of this illustration still today. I have shared much of the criticism of Hromadka for being so one-sided in his attitude toward Communism. The worst example was his acceptance of the official Communist defense of the suppression of the Hungarian revolution. Yet I am sure that this illustration reflects the real Hromadka, that his political positions have never involved identifi-

The second illustration is more familiar, and also more instructive because it comes from the experience of one who had decisive political responsibility—the experience of Abraham Lincoln. It has often been said that Lincoln was not an orthodox Christian, and doubtless he was critical of the conventional theology that he knew. But he was a man of profound biblical faith, and it would be difficult to find in history a better example of a Christian statesman who did not allow his scruples to destroy his sense of responsibility for determined action and who did not allow his sense of responsibility for determined action to destroy his charity or his humility. The contrast between the Christian spirit in politics and the Communist spirit in politics can be seen embodied in the contrast between Lincoln and Lenin. Both were men of integrity who served causes that could claim high moral sanction. Berdyaev says of Lenin:

> Lenin was not a vicious man; there was a great deal of good in him; he was unmercenary, absolutely devoted to an idea; he was not even a particularly ambitious man or a great lover of power; he thought but little of himself; but the sole obsession of a single idea led to a dreadful narrowing of thought and to a moral transformation which permitted entirely immoral methods of carrying out the conflict.[11]

The chief difference between Lenin and Lincoln was that for Lenin the cause was everything, while for Lincoln the purpose and judgment of God, which in ways

---

cation of the Christian faith with Communism, that he has preserved in his own mind much theological and religious tension between his faith and his politics. For a fair estimate, see Charles C. West, *Communism and the Theologians* (Philadelphia: The Westminster Press, 1958), pp. 57–77.

11 *Origin of Russian Communism*, p. 140.

beyond human understanding embraced both sides in the conflict, transcended even his cause. As a consequence of this, Lincoln's enemies, whom he had to fight and to whose sufferings he could never become callous, were always the objects of his charity.

The Ultimate Status of Persons

There is a third conflict between Christianity and Communism which really underlies the second but I want to give it emphasis in concluding this discussion of the issues between Christianity and Communism. This is a conflict over the status of the human person. There has been some ambiguity about this in original Marxist thought, and perhaps even now this ambiguity is implicit in what Communists believe concerning the ideal society. The original Marxist dream pointed to a society in which persons would be emancipated from the specific shackles that history had put upon them. There is much said in Marx's early writings about the estrangement from himself that man has experienced as a result of oppressive social and economic systems. Engels looked for the time when humanity would "leap from the realm of necessity to the realm of freedom."[12] The anarchistic belief in the withering away of the state presupposes the expectation of greater freedom for the person. But, true as all this may be, there has been a tendency in Communism to lose interest in the dignity and freedom of the person. The materialistic and deterministic categories of thought have had a depersonalizing effect upon the spirit of Communism. The inevitable preoccupation with the problems of the masses and the long years of revolution and dictatorship when the person is necessarily sacrificed

---

[12] *Anti-Duhring*, p. 310.

to the community have had the same effect. Communism does not have an adequate frame of reference to provide an understanding of the conditions on which the dignity of the person depends. There are depths of personal life that are beyond the comprehension of those who concentrate exclusively on social forces, historical processes, and systems of production.

Christianity combines, in a remarkable way, concern for the uniqueness and ultimate worth of every person with concern for the community of persons. There is a radical individualism in the gospel, with its assurance that "even the hairs of your head are numbered" (Matthew 10:30), with its faith that God cares about the single sheep that is lost (Matthew 18:12–14), with its warning against the despising of "one of these little ones" (Matthew 18:10). The love that is central in the whole New Testament is love directed toward individual persons, and yet it is love that binds them together into a community. The radical individualism of the gospel is closely united with emphasis upon the Kingdom and upon the Church which, against the background of the Old Testament preparation, have a very strong social reference.

A recent analysis of the status of the individual person by Jacques Maritain expresses admirably the interrelationship between the person and the community. Maritain says:

> Man finds himself by subordinating himself to the group; the group attains its goal only by serving man and by realizing that man has secrets which escape the group and a vocation which the group does not encompass.[13]

---

[13] Jacques Maritain, *The Rights of Man and Natural Law* (New York: Charles Scribner's Sons, 1943), p. 18.

In order to make clearer the issue between Christianity and Communism at this point, I shall suggest various ways in which the role of the individual person in the perspective of Christian faith is understood. The false individualisms that have plagued modern society and that have helped to produce as a reaction the one-sided collectivism of Communism are often enough criticized elsewhere in this book.

As the background for everything else that should be said is the conviction that the status of the individual person depends upon the love of God. There are many reasons why persons of obvious dignity and worth should be respected, but these reasons break down when persons lose their obvious dignity and worth. They may lose their status in this sense when they seem morally lost or when they become shiftless non-producers or when they become enemies or opponents of our nation or class or cause. But the Christian gospel stands or falls with the faith in the aggressive love of God for those who do not deserve it on any human basis. One of the key sentences in the New Testament is Paul's surprising claim: "But God shows his love for us in that while we were yet sinners Christ died for us" (Romans 5:8). In the Christian understanding of God's dealing with men, those words of Paul indicate the actual divine implementation on a universal scale of the idea expressed in the gospel parables of the lost sheep and the prodigal son. Communism knows nothing about such teaching as this. The opponent becomes an outcast "fascist," "warmonger," or "reactionary" and that is the end of the matter until the day comes when through the working out of the historical process, after numerous purges and liquidations, there is a world in which there are no opponents. But all of the opponents who have stood in the way in the course of this development are lost souls and for them there is no redemption.

Against this background there are other signs of the status of the person that can be pointed out in the Christian view of things.

The individual person is the ultimate unit of moral and religious decision. No one else can repent for him. No one else can respond in faith to the truth in his place. No one else can assume his moral responsibility. No external authority can create in him conscience or moral insight or that inner awareness of what is good on which his judgments depend. This is one of the reasons why Christians must seek the kind of spiritual freedom that leaves air for the person to breathe and in which it is externally possible for the truth to be accepted or rejected.

The individual person's status is supported by Christian teaching about the ultimate destiny of the person. Ideas of resurrection and of immortality emphasize the permanence of the person and exclude all conceptions of the loss of the person in some absolute being.

It was in an individual person, not in a nation or community or class or any other social group, in whom, as Christians believe, the Word was made flesh and dwelt among us. It is highly significant that Christians have always seen the supreme revelation of God and the supreme action of God in human life in an individual person.

In the light of these ways of thinking of the status of the person, it is natural for Christians to believe that all doctrines and all ways of organizing human society are wrong that lead to a situation in which the person is a mere creature of the state. Any doctrine or society is wrong in which the subordination of the individual to the welfare of the community is not corrected by the belief that the welfare of the community has no meaning outside the experience of individual persons. And, for Christians, there is the recognition that the test of that welfare must include the increasing depth and richness and freedom of personal life.

5

The Christian Contribution

WHAT ARE the elements in the Christian religion which contribute to the solution of the very problems which drive many of our contemporaries to embrace Communism?

Often in the previous chapters I have assumed that there is a Christian social imperative that is as radical as the social imperative in Communism. On what is the Christian social imperative based? How can we account for the social conservatism that has so generally characterized the Christian churches if their own faith implies such an imperative?

The basis of the Christian social imperative may be seen both in God's purpose for his creation and in the meaning of Christian love. These are two approaches to the same reality. God is the Lord of humanity, of its public affairs as well as of the personal life of each individual. The Christian life is lived under the command to do the will of God. God, as we know him through the Bible, is no abstract principle, no far-off deity, but the active Creator and Redeemer of the world. In Luke's Gospel, before the account of the birth of Jesus we have this prophecy that sums up the expectation that prepared the way for Christianity: "Blessed be the Lord God of Israel, for he has visited and redeemed his people, and has raised up a horn of salvation for us in the house of his servant David" (Luke 1:68–69). This was the expectant faith, and though it was often limited in its perspective to the people of Israel, Israel was regarded by its greatest sons as the bearer of salvation to all mankind.

The response to that expectation is given in a later affirmation that reflects the faith of the Church: "And the Word became flesh and dwelt among us, full of grace and truth; and we have beheld his glory, glory of the only Son from the Father" (John 1:14). The deepest conviction that underlies this expectation and this faith in its fulfillment is the conviction that God is with man in history—that God has not left the world to run itself or to be run by men but that he seeks to deliver men from the many forms of bondage in which they are held, from the bondage in which they hold one another. Here are the words of Jesus which Luke records as his first message and which, quoted as they are from the book of Isaiah, convey to us the imperative in the Old Testament:

> The Spirit of the Lord is upon me,
> because he has anointed me to preach good news to
>   the poor.
> He has sent me to proclaim release to the captives
> and recovering of sight to the blind,
> to set at liberty those who are oppressed,
> to proclaim the acceptable year of the Lord.
>
> Luke 4:18–19

God, as known to us through Christ, seeks a community that is favorable to the real welfare of all of his children. What stands out most clearly as the social meaning of the New Testament teaching about God's purpose for man is that all groups of human beings are equally the objects of the love and concern of God. If there is inequality in the divine concern for men, it is the kind that undercuts all of our human schemes of inequality—it is God's special concern for the lost sheep, for those whom the world has discarded.

This affirmation about God's equal concern for all groups of human beings may seem platitudinous, but think what it means if we follow it out consistently. It means that all of the ways in which the privileged few have exploited and lorded it over the masses of men throughout history are an offense to God. It means that it is intolerable that there should be any persons, any groups of persons, who are the victims of policies or systems by which we profit or to which we consent. It means that every child has the same right as every other child to the conditions that are favorable to his development as a person, the right to be free from malnutrition, from the humiliation of racial discrimination and segregation, the right to have access to the means of health and education. It means that whatever may be said about the importance of avoiding a dead level of equality either in income or status because of the varieties of function that must be performed and because of the requirements for incentive, all such differences should be relative and provisional and should not be allowed to harden and to create chasms between social classes.

We come to the same result if we approach it by way of the implications of Christian love. The love of the neighbor must include the struggle for a social order that is favorable to the real welfare of all neighbors. This in the Christian life involves compassion and the willingness to sacrifice one's own advantage for the achievement of that end. We have a special responsibility for all, whether they are near or far, whose lives are affected by our own decisions. Christian love cannot be limited to purely personal relations; it must include caring for the people whom we have never seen and whom we cannot imagine as individual persons. As I have said in the last chapter, Christian love includes concern for the real welfare of enemies and opponents. There are no limits to its range and there are no limits to the willingness to sacrifice which such love implies.

Christian churches have often in the past been so otherworldly, or so conservative, or so individualistic, that they have done little more than give religious sanction to the *status quo* or to the interests of the classes dominant within them. How can this be explained if what I have said about the social meaning of Christian love is true? There are two types of explanation and each involves a very long story. One calls attention to the sociological factors that have made it natural for churches, since the time of Constantine, to accommodate themselves to the institutions of the world, partly because of the sheer pressure of the world upon them and partly because of the desire to be in a position to discipline the world and to minister in a religious way to whole nations.

The other type of explanation calls attention to elements in Christian faith itself which when given emphasis in a context of one-sided interpretations have led to serious distortions. Concentration on otherworldly expectations can lead to an escape from social responsibility if it is separated from faith that God is working out his purposes in human history. Concentration on divine providence in a world of relatively static institutions can lead Christians to accept the existing institutions as ordained by God and may discourage all efforts at revolutionary change. Concentration on the ways in which the individual soul strengthened by faith in Christ can "do all things" may divert attention from the plight of unknown masses of humanity who, before they grow into maturity or spiritual freedom, are blocked by external circumstances that are beyond their control. Concentration upon love in purely personal terms may lead to the illusion that all social problems can be solved by a well-meaning paternalism that never questions the existing location of power or the existing distribution of wealth. Concentration upon a perfectionist understanding of the ways in which love must be expressed may make it impossible to think in terms of effective political action.

More important than this analysis of the reasons for past weaknesses of the Church in this area is the story of what has happened in most of the branches of the Church in the past half century. There has been an extraordinary change of climate in the churches. The conservative and individualistic distortions of Christianity have very generally lost their hold upon the churches and new movements for Christian social action have grown up in most of the churches, Catholic and Protestant. I do not mean that the rank and file of Christians do not still, in considerable measure, represent the conventional assumptions of their nation or class, but what has happened is that the change in thought and in commitment on the part of those who exercise leadership has been so marked that the churches are moving in a new direction.

This tendency to stress the social responsibility of the Christian and of the Church was at first most influential in Britain and America and in the churches of mission lands most influenced by Anglo-Saxon Christianity. But in recent years, partly as a result of the necessity of political resistance to National Socialism, the churches on the European continent have become very much aware of their social responsibility. Leaders of the churches on the European continent are more active in progressive politics than is the case in this country. Influential thinkers in the contemporary Church are deeply committed to Christian social action. In quite different ways this is true of Karl Barth, of Reinhold Niebuhr, of Emil Brunner, of Paul Tillich; and it was true of Archbishop William Temple and of Nicolas Berdyaev. The World Council of Churches which came into existence at its Amsterdam Assembly in August, 1948, and which is the official organ of most of the branches of the Church except Roman Catholicism, is deeply committed to this same understanding of Christian responsibility. There has been a parallel tendency in the Roman Church since the great social encyclicals of Pope Leo XIII, and in industrialized countries where Roman Catholicism is not too much handicapped by its ties with a continuing feudalism it is often progressive in its economic teaching and policies.[1]

It may make this development more comprehensible to call attention to some of the reasons for it. The fact of

---

[1] The trend that I have been outlining has continued on a world scale. The Second Assembly of the World Council of Churches in 1954 in Evanston put as much emphasis on social issues as the First Assembly in Amsterdam. In many branches of the Church there is more stress on the problem of racial justice than ever before. In the United States there is a combination of complacency about economic issues and a sense of the complexity of international issues that prevents the formation of decisive positions. In the churches of Asia there is more awareness of social issues than ever before. There may, as I write, be more social indifference in the United States than in 1948, but there has been no great change in the trend described in the text at the level of theological thought or at the level of church organization.

momentous changes in the world and in particular the fall of the old regimes that claimed religious sanctions and the rise of new classes to power have at least discredited the static conceptions of divine providence. The fact that the working classes and the colored races have become articulate and organized for both moral and political pressure has forced the more comfortable classes to recognize the needs, the aspirations, and the potentialities of the vast masses of humanity which have been neglected or exploited. The old illusions that have enabled Christians to assume that they should exercise irresponsible economic or political power over others for *their* sake have become untenable except to the minds of the most hide-bound. There is great educative power in a *fait accompli,* and the more conservative groups in many countries, including our own, now accept as a matter of course practices that they formerly regarded with horror as "socialistic." Perhaps most important has been the way in which the alternatives that face the world have been narrowed by modern developments, so that we see that Christians must now take responsibility to work for an ordered economy with full employment and a far more equal distribution of wealth in order to avoid the destructive effects of economic depressions; for the perfecting of the institutions of world community in order to avoid atomic destruction; for a democratic order that is able to combine social justice with political and cultural freedom in order to avoid an oppressive tyranny.

The events of our time which reveal the providence of God, his judgment and his promise, in a way that was hidden from Christians who lived in other and more static periods, have completely demolished the illusion that the white man who happened to belong to the more privileged classes in Europe or America could muddle along with a few concessions to the rest of humanity but with no radical changes in the institutions that were so satisfying to his economic interests and his pride.

I have emphasized great historical forces which have changed the minds of Christians. This may seem to resemble the Communist argument that the religious ideas and institutions are reflections of social realities which alone have substance. There is just enough truth in this Communist claim to make it plausible. Men's visions and ideals are conditioned to a great degree by the social forces that press upon them. I do not believe, for one moment, that those in our time who see more clearly than their fathers the social meaning of Christianity are more devout or more sincerely committed Christians than their fathers. There is a continuous thread in the Christian movement of genuine devotion to Christ that every generation should acknowledge. But when the external alternatives that face Christians change, they learn something about God's will for them that may have been hidden from previous generations. They would not respond to these events with Christian repentance and Christian love if they did not bring to them what they have received from their faith. They are free to choose even now between a Christian response and a Communist response or between a Christian response and the response of the cynical reactionary. So, there is no simple historical determinism but rather real interaction between what Christians bring to their situation from the distinctive Christian revelation of God's purpose and the illumination that comes from the events and the historical forces which surround them, events and historical forces which, to the eyes of faith, also reveal the purpose of God.

So far I have stressed the fact that Christianity shares with Communism its concern for the changing of social institutions in the interests of more equal justice, in the interests of the classes and races which are their victims. But when we go deeper into what this means in practice, we find that Christians are not able to identify their Christian goal unreservedly with particular political and economic programs for attaining it.

The Christian, as a Christian, ought to know what his goal and what his motive should be. He should be in a position to see what is wrong with existing institutions and he should be able to understand himself, his own temptation to be influenced by his own interests and those of his social group. He should be guided by a faith that enables him to live with confidence in the mercy and in the ultimate victory of God even in times when it would be natural to despair. But there is a gap here that Christians cannot fill from Christian resources alone, and that is the choice of the technical or the political means that are essential in any complete program of action. They must keep all means under criticism and some they should, as Christians, reject, but there are open questions in this area to which there are no absolute Christian answers.

Communism as an authoritarian movement is able to supply full guidance to the individual, though the guidance is subject to sudden and embarrassing changes. Roman Catholicism has the capacity to give more guidance for social action than Protestantism because only an authoritarian system is able to give assurance concerning the next step to be taken in a complex and rapidly changing world. The Christian must frankly say that the kingdom of God is not identical with any social institutions or any political program. He knows that he lives in a mixed society in which only a minority are committed to Christian standards. He knows that the alternatives between which he must choose are limited and that all of them are morally ambiguous because of the corporate sin and finiteness which he himself shares. The Protestant should be especially wary of allowing church authority to make evil appear good or to give a special blessing to institutions or policies in which the Church itself may have a vested interest as a human community.

In the long run it is an advantage that Christians as Christians cannot claim to have all of the answers. If they identified the kingdom of God with a particular social system and with the means by which it is established and maintained, they would be constantly confusing the absolute and the relative, they would tend to freeze some new *status quo* and to become subject to the illusion that in defending it they were defending God. If the New Testament gave us a social program, including both ends and means, it would have been out of date long ago. Instead it gives us the perspective from which to judge all social programs and it constrains us to find the best possible program in each particular situation.

Instead of assuming that the kingdom of God is identical with any particular social cause, we can say that we serve the kingdom of God by serving the cause that seems most fully to embody God's purpose for us. The kingdom transcends all causes, and yet there are causes that point toward it and there are causes that point away from it.

The individual Christian needs the help of other Christians when he is faced with difficult decisions, and the Church should be a community in which collective guidance that does not claim to be absolute can give him aid. This collective guidance depends for its value upon the participation of those who have expert knowledge or who have responsibility for concrete decisions. The churches have begun to create channels for just that kind of guidance. In the last part of this chapter I shall give some examples of how the Church has sought to provide collective Christian guidance on social problems. There have been many other examples of this in recent years. I do not refer to the casual resolutions passed by church assemblies that are called primarily for other purposes, but to the work of commissions and conferences which have concentrated on specific controversial issues. One of the most significant was the Conference at Oxford on the Church, Community, and State in 1937, which came as close as any representative group of Christians have come in our time to the defining of the objectives that should guide Christians in political and economic life.[2]

One understands very little about Christianity if one considers the social imperative alone. The Christian social imperative, and indeed the Christian ethic in general, comes to us in a context which gives it an ultimate meaning that is lacking in all movements that are directed only to the transformation of society. This context provides essential correctives to the ways in which men seek to realize justice and brotherhood in history. This other dimension of Christian faith is sure to lead to serious distortions if it is not kept in the closest relation with the tasks that are set by the social imperative. There are many ways of suggesting the difference between the two dimensions of Christianity which are here in view. They may be classified as religious and ethical, or vertical

---

[2] I have discussed more fully the difficulties that we confront in the case of political and economic decisions, and the nature of the guidance that is available in the Church, in *Christian Ethics and Social Policy* (New York: Charles Scribner's Sons, 1946).

and horizontal, or otherworldly and this-worldly, or eternal and temporal dimensions, or as the dimensions of faith and works. All of these contrasts too readily prepare the way for the separation of the dimensions which instead should interact in Christian thought and life. Even the word "dimension" is a metaphor which suggests separation.

Whatever we may call the two dimensions of Christianity, they are not to be separated, and in a real sense the ethical or social dimension is a test of the soundness of the grasp of any Christian or of any Christian Church upon the more distinctively religious dimension. "For he who does not love his brother whom he has seen, cannot love God whom he has not seen" (1 John 4:20). That is the ethical test of religion, but the words which precede indicate that in a sense religion is prior to ethics: "We love because he first loved us" (1 John 4:19).

I shall now present some of the elements in Christianity which may seem to many who are interested in the problems with which Communism deals to be, at best, so much traditional baggage or, at worst, a source of diversion or escape from the main task. However, these elements actually provide a context of meaning and correction which is lacking in a movement or faith that knows only the one dimension to which social action belongs.

Christian teaching about human nature perhaps reveals most clearly the corrective elements in Christianity. It corrects all tendencies toward sentimental optimism or utopianism that fail to prepare men to face the stubborn reality of evil in human history, and it corrects all tendencies to disillusionment or cynicism that are the opposite danger. Men who lack the perspective of Christian teaching are in danger of oscillating between utopianism and disillusionment.

The first thing that Christians say about human nature is that man—and this means every man—is made in the image of God and that this image is the basis of man's dignity and promise.

The second thing that Christians say about human nature is that man—and this means every man and not merely those who are opponents or enemies—is a sinner.

The word "sinner" often proves a great obstacle to understanding, but let us use other words. Let us say that man is the kind of creature who naturally sees the world from a very limited perspective, that he tends to be self-centered, to prefer the interests that are closest to himself and to his own social group. Let us say that man is naturally unwilling to accept his limited or finite status, that he is always seeking to extend his control over others, that he seeks to maintain his own security by means of power over all who may threaten it, that he likes to be in a position to compare himself with others to their disadvantage, that he seeks to be self-sufficient and to deny in effect his dependence upon God and to set up his own group or system or ideal in the place of God.

Is there any denying that self-centeredness and pride are natural to man? Because of the religious dimension of Christianity we see this self-centeredness and pride not only in words or overt acts or in social institutions; the Christian sees them in his own motives and attitudes before God who searcheth the heart; he sees them in himself against a standard of love and integrity of motive that he meets only in Christ.

The positive side of Christian teaching about man, the belief that all men are made in God's image, is the corrective for cynicism even when things are at their worst, when forces of hate and violence seem to have covered up most of the good in human life. It is also the ultimate source of hope for society. This hope is not based upon man's innate powers but on the belief that man never ceases to be the kind of being who can be renewed by the grace of God or the spirit of God.

Man never ceases to be a responsible being and no mere victim of circumstance or of the consequences of the sins of his fathers. Man has the amazing capacity through memory and thought and imagination to transcend himself and his own time and place, to criticize himself and his environment on the basis of ideals and purposes that are present to his mind, and he can aspire in the grimmest situations to realize these ideals and purposes in his personal life and in society. It is this capacity for self-transcendence that Reinhold Niebuhr, following Augustine, regards as the chief mark of the image of God in man that is never lost. Man is made for the highest, to respond in worship and loyalty to God himself, and it is one of the evidences of man's greatness that he soon knows frustration, sickness of the soul, or catastrophes in his civilizations when he makes anything less than the highest the end of his existence.

Every word that Christians say about the sin of man or about the darkness of his life is an indirect claim that man is uniquely great among all creatures, for only responsible beings with great gifts and powers could fall to such depths or cause such vast destruction. Pascal, who emphasized both the greatness and the misery of man and who saw the interdependence of that greatness and that misery, had a profound grasp of the Christian view of the human problem. In Pascal's *Thoughts* there are many passages that bring out the interdependence of man's greatness and man's misery. Here are a few examples:

The greatness of man is great in that he knows himself to be miserable. A tree does not know itself to be miserable.

All these same miseries prove man's greatness. They are the miseries of a great lord, of a deposed king.

All that the one party has been able to say in proof of his [man's] greatness has only served as an argument of his wretchedness to the others, because the greater our fall, the more wretched we are, and *vice versa*.[3]

Such a view of man as this should be enough to show how false it is to think of man as no more than a creature who can be useful to some political cause or who is defined only by his relation to a class, a party, or a state.

The emphasis upon the possibilities of man enables the Christian to have hope for the future of society. He should reject any doctrine of progress that promises complete, inevitable, or secure progress or that finds the full meaning of our present existence in future achievements. But he should also reject dogmatic pessimism or dark fatalism about the future. Reinhold Niebuhr, known popularly for his warnings against false hopes, has stated the faith in an open future. Frequently he says that there are "indeterminate possibilities" in human history. He says:

There are no limits to be set in history for the achievement of a more universal brotherhood, for the development of more perfect and more inclusive human relations. All the characteristic hopes and aspirations of Renaissance and Enlightenment, of both secular and Christian liberalism are right at least in this, that they understand that side of Christian doctrine which regards the *agape* of the King-

---

[3] Blaise Pascal, *Thoughts,* Everyman's Library Edition (New York: E. P. Dutton & Co., 1951), pp. 397, 398, 416.

dom of God as a resource for infinite developments toward
a more perfect brotherhood in history.[4]

But Dr. Niebuhr is also right in his oft-repeated warning that the most dangerous threat to such human advances is the tendency to believe that one's own group has
either achieved the ideal or possesses the secret of its
achievement.

Christian teaching concerning the depth and persistence of sin is a necessary corrective for all political and
social movements. I have emphasized the conviction that
it is the lack of any such understanding of human nature
that is the source of Communism's greatest errors. Guided
by Christian teaching we can always be on our guard
against two destructive tendencies. We can be on our
guard against the self-righteousness that makes men blind
to the failures of their own nation or class or party and
that usually increases the bitterness of group conflict. Is
there any other influence except the influence of Christian faith that causes men to begin by confessing their
own sins rather than the sins of their opponents? Only a
habit of drastic self-criticism will prepare many people to
see the subtle ways in which their opinions and their
votes are influenced by the narrow interests of the social
groups to which they belong.

The second tendency which Christian teaching about
human nature should help us to guard against is the
tendency to assume that some advance in culture or in
technical skill or in social organization will be secure
against the old evils that come from the love of money or
power or the desire to have someone else upon whom
we can look down. It is possible to overcome in consid-

---

[4] Reinhold Niebuhr, *The Nature and Destiny of Man* (New
York: Charles Scribner's Sons, 1943), Vol. II, p. 85.

erable measure these old evils but they are sure to reappear in new forms the moment we believe that we are secure against them. Christians themselves need to be aware of the forms of these old evils that are likely to corrupt the life of the Church or the life of any "Christian civilization" if it is taught by the Church to claim too much for itself.[5]

Turn now to the center of Christianity, to the gospel of the forgiving love of God. This has been expressed in the great Protestant traditions in terms of the doctrine of justification by faith alone. Strange as much of this terminology is to most of our contemporaries, it deals with realities which correspond to their own needs. There is a universal hunger of the human spirit to have right relations with, or to be accepted by, whatever one regards as having ultimate authority. This hunger is often enough concealed by distracting activities and it often receives satisfaction for a time from various forms of social approval. But the more reflective and sensitive one is and the more one sees through the claims to authority of the world's idols, the greater need of being "justified" by God. The most obvious way of gaining such "justification" is through the effort to earn it by moral and religious works, but, again, the more reflective and sensitive one is, the more it becomes apparent that no works are really good enough. It is the heart of the Christian gospel that God will accept us as we are if only we begin to be open toward him, if only we receive with faith what he has done for all men, including ourselves, through Christ. Here it is important to realize that faith is not intellectual

---

[5] Readers would do well to consult Chapter VII of Reinhold Niebuhr's first volume of *The Nature and Destiny of Man*. That chapter describes with amazing penetration the various ways in which spirits of men on all levels are distorted by pride.

belief but what I call, for lack of better words, the beginning of openness toward God. This gospel received its first full expression in Paul's epistles. Here are two of their greatest sentences which give the substance of it: "But God shows his love toward us in that while we were yet sinners Christ died for us" (Romans 5:8). "For by grace you have been saved through faith; and this is not your own doing, it is the gift of God—not because of works, lest any man should boast" (Ephesians 2:8–9).

At first sight this central element in Christian teaching and Christian life would seem to be most irrelevant to all the problems with which Communism deals. But actually it has great importance for them, though it was wrought out and expressed by Paul and Luther in a quite different context, the context of the deepest inner spiritual struggles. We can see the social relevance of this gospel of forgiveness if we realize that one of the ways in which men do seek to gain right relations with or acceptance by whatever is most authoritative for them is through the attempt to realize ideals in society, to earn their own status before God or their nation or their class or "history" by such striving.

This effort may take the form of the struggle for a life of perfect love in the world, and this has often, in the case of Christians, led to withdrawal from the political order as too much stained by violence or coercion or by compromises of absolute honesty. This behavior, while it is quite explicable and while it may make a positive contribution to society if too many people are not drawn toward it, involves real irresponsibility because it leaves the dirty work of the world to others. Those who seek greater personal purity in this manner must themselves live off the compromises of others who continue to take responsibility for the institutions of the world in the interests of order and justice and production. A better understanding of Christianity would enable such people to take any necessary role in the world's life and trust, not in their own precarious righteousness, but in the grace of God for their "justification."

A far more dangerous result of the effort to win ultimate spiritual security or justification (what is often intended by the extraordinarily popular phrase "peace of mind") appears when men make a furious effort to deceive themselves concerning their own moral achievement. They do this by making their opponents the moral scapegoats and pour upon them the hostility that may have its origin in their own disguised moral insecurity. They do this by attaching themselves to some movement or program or cause and then convincing themselves that this movement or program or cause is the embodiment of the ideal. The more they feel insecure within, the more they must stretch what truth there may be in their claims for their cause. They justify themselves by justifying their cause. If they happen to have political power and the capacity to force their will upon others, we have all of the violent short cuts that are characteristic of Communism. Communism is unaware of the deep hunger of the human spirit which the Christian gospel can satisfy, but it does provide an unconscious solution of the problem that it fails to recognize. But in doing this it lays the groundwork for the most dangerous self-deception and the most cruel fanaticism.

The gospel of forgiveness and the warning against self-deception that accompanies it have been most often associated with the name of Paul, but there was never a more vivid expression of it, one that immediately carries conviction, than Jesus' parable of the Pharisee and the publican:

He also told this parable to some who trusted in themselves that they were righteous and despised others: "Two men went up into the temple to pray, one a Pharisee and the other a tax collector. The Pharisee stood and prayed thus with himself: 'God, I thank thee that I am not like other men, extortioners, unjust, adulterers, or even like this tax collector. I fast twice a week, I give tithes of all that I get.' But the tax collector, standing far off, would not even lift up his eyes to heaven, but beat his breast, saying: 'God, be merciful to me a sinner!' I tell you, this man went down to his house justified rather than the other; for everyone who exalts himself will be humbled, but he who humbles himself will be exalted." (Luke 18:9–14, R.S.V.)

This gospel enables the Christian to do whatever seems to be required of him in the world, in the political order as much as in what may seem to be the morally safer areas of private life, in the knowledge that God will accept him in spite of the evil in which his actions involve him. This can be stated in such a way as to relax moral standards, but that is to miss the remarkable paradox of Christian teaching which makes men acutely sensitive to the claims of the moral standard while it promises forgiveness.

This gospel frees men to do the best that they know how and yet to do so without self-deception and without the self-righteous defensiveness which is itself the source of moral blindness. To do the best that one can and yet to know that one's ultimate standing before God depends only upon his mercy and not upon one's own moral success is also the beginning of charity in life's hardest situations, charity toward enemies and opponents who stand under the same mercy. Those who stress only the moral law are in danger of becoming loveless and unforgiving and thus to transgress the law itself.

This gospel, which seems so strange because of the popular ignorance of the meaning of the words in which it is expressed, and which seems so repellent to many because of its use by some Christians as a substitute for moral striving, is the teaching that is most needed by Christians who are tortured by the moral dilemmas in which they find themselves and who only wish that they might postpone all decisions until they are in a quite new situation. That quite new situation is likely to be elusive, and if it appears in sight it is likely to be found not so different from the old.

I should say again that this gospel is not intended to help anyone follow the line of least resistance with an easy conscience. Only those can know what its meaning is who have experienced what it is to be *so* cornered that *every* alternative open to them threatens their inner moral security.

Closely linked with the gospel of forgiveness is another contribution of Christianity, also an indirect one, to the solution of social problems. It is what I am calling "the ultimate hope." It is the conviction that what we do or achieve does not have its total meaning in terms of observable historical results, that all that has gone into it of faith and honest commitment to God's kingdom will be used by God in ways that are beyond our calculation. It is the faith that death does not defeat the purposes of God in personal life but that new life beyond death is our personal destiny. It is the faith that the destruction of a civilization, even the total destruction of human life on this planet, would not defeat God. In the days before the release of atomic energy it was psychologically possible to base faith for action upon expectations for the distant future, even though the distant future might be closed by a cosmic catastrophe so remote that it caused no serious concern. But now, whatever the future may have in store for us, there is no doubt that all that we live for in this world is insecure.

This emphasis upon the ultimate hope can be abused and become the otherworldliness that has caused many to reject Christianity as an escape religion unrelated to the problems of society. But there is an otherworldly perspective that is essential for sanity in the case of anyone who is not self-deceived about the actual human situation. It is not likely, in the case of contemporary Christianity, that those who share this perspective will become so sure in their grasp upon the details of any ultimate fulfillment that they will lose their concern to make the best of conditions in this world. This otherworldliness should release the Christian from the panic or paralysis that may come upon those who find the whole meaning of their lives within the limits of history. This will help us to avoid both cynicism and despair. This will enable us to carry on after many social movements and panaceas have brought disillusionment to their adherents. Christianity has already survived many such confident gospels, because it is oriented strongly toward our historical existence and yet looks beyond toward God's kingdom that will bring to fulfillment what is in accordance with his purpose in all our strivings and in all our achievements. There was a time when faith in God for many modern Christians depended in part upon the empirical grounds for hope concerning our future in this world. But today I believe that the situation is reversed and that what hope we may have for our future in this world will depend upon a prior faith that this is God's world and that he is Lord of its future.

To say these things may, at first, suggest to those who are not convinced Christians that Christians easily believe what is beyond evidence. Such an ultimate faith becomes credible only when we contrast it with the alternative assumption, which is most likely to take its place, that the end of our historical existence as a race will be the end of all that has been thought or loved in the experience of men, that it will leave no trace, not even a memory that there had ever been anything to remember. Such a nihilistic assumption, if we live with it long, becomes incredible; and the more so, if ever we have taken seriously other aspects of the Christian faith in God as known through Jesus Christ. But even then many Christians must say of these final convictions: "I believe, help thou my unbelief."

These last two elements in Christianity—the gospel of forgiveness and the ultimate hope—become fully meaningful only when men face the depths in personal life or almost reach the limit of endurance in their social situation. As long as one is able to be morally satisfied with the best available choices and as long as a society can see far ahead with no dark shadows on the way, it is possible to dispense with them. But the prospect of the death of the individual is a reminder of the human limits that we try to forget. And today there are many places in the world in which it would be impossible to carry on at all without either fanatical devotion to a political program like Communism that by the rapidity with which it generates self-deceptions serves to hide our limitations, or a faith like Christianity that sees the best and the worst in human life in relation to God's purpose. In the long run any faith for life will be tested by its fitness for the deepest places and the hardest situations.

After reviewing the Christian view of human nature,

the gospel of forgiveness, and the ultimate hope, we are in a position to see in a broad way one of the most distinctive aspects of Christianity, its way of dealing with the many-sided evil in human life. It may be useful to put together in a few words this Christian approach to evil, because in the long run it is likely that this will prove to be decisive in the conflict between Christianity and Communism as conceptions of life. Communism's weakest point is that it underestimates the reality of evil and so puts its confidence in too simple a solution of the human problem.

Christianity does not seek to cover up the fact of evil now or in the future. It knows no revolution in history that will fully overcome it. Its teaching about human nature is realistic in its recognition of the universality and persistence of sin in our personal and collective life. It does not make any promises concerning an earthly utopia that will be brought about by human action. The kingdom of God sets for us our tasks but it stands above all of our achievements. Also, the central symbol of Christianity is the Cross of Christ, a perpetual reminder of the results of the sin and blindness of men. Christianity is a religion of redemption for those who by faith live in the midst of the world with all of its sin and tragedy. It is not a religion that assures us of fair weather. Many of our contemporaries have rediscovered the truth and relevance of Christianity because only in its gospel have they found a word that was deep enough or healing enough for them in the world as it is.

Christianity does not explain evil away. It discourages self-deception concerning evil. It teaches no fatalism about evil, for it sees the responsibility of man under the sovereignty of God. It inspires us to seek to overcome evil in ourselves and in the world, and its gospel of forgiveness and its ultimate hope enable us to live with faith amidst the evil that is not overcome.

There have been one-sided forms of Christianity, often popular distortions rather than the teachings of the great theologians. Some of these distortions have stressed the divine sovereignty to the neglect of human responsibility for evil; others have stressed forgiveness as though it were a substitute for moral growth; still others have stressed the ultimate hope as though it took the place of the effort to realize justice in the social order. And there have been theologies that were the reverse of all of these. But Christianity can be rightly understood only when all of these convictions are held together.

It cannot be too much emphasized that Christianity is not primarily a system of ideas but a living movement in the world that traces its origin to particular events in human history. I have indicated that in this respect there is a formal similarity between Christianity and Communism, though they differ profoundly in content.

Christianity is the faith that the turning point in human history was the coming of Jesus Christ as the one who has decisively mediated God to men, as the one who in his life and death and victory over death brought into the world a new community. It will seem to many readers an anticlimax to identify that new community as the Christian Church, for they have seen some examples of Christian churches. I do not say, without qualification, that the new community is the Church, if, by Church, we think of the concrete institutions and congregations which bear that name. But it remains true that it is chiefly through these same institutions and congregations that the new community becomes embodied. It has been their work to transmit from generation to generation the Bible through which God speaks to men his clearest word, and they have formed the banks between which the continuous stream of Christian life has moved until it reaches us. The Church is an earthen vessel that carries the greatest treasure and it is an indispensable vessel if the treasure is to come near us. It is a great difficulty for some Christians to prevent the most rigorous criticism of the earthen vessel from hiding the treasure, and for others to prevent the treasure from giving a false glow of sanctity to the earthen vessel.

Already in this book I have said a great deal in criticism of the Church. I have emphasized the conviction that Communism in its criticism of the bourgeois world and in its emphasis upon economic justice has brought to the Church an essential corrective. The Church has often gone far astray in its teaching and attitudes in relation to the social order. But there is one saving fact about the Church. It is not its own Lord or its own judge. The Church, when it is true to itself, sees itself under the Lordship and under the judgment of Christ. It is also an essential factor that the revelation of God's purpose for the Church comes to it through the Bible and is therefore independent of the "ideologies" of its own members. So, when the Church feels great pressure from outside, as it has done in the case of the whole movement of social radicalism, of which Communism is only an extreme expression, it finds that this pressure corresponds in part to the demands of its own Lord.

Today the most searching criticisms of the Church come from within. They hit the mark more surely than the more ignorant and stereotyped criticisms that usually come from outside. The Church is now going through a period of the most rigorous self-examination and it sees more clearly than at any time in the modern period the need for a radical reformation. It is because of this that it is possible to speak with confidence of the Christian community within the churches and to regard it as the tangible result in history of the new beginning that can be traced to the coming of Christ.

What does the fact of this Christian community within the churches mean for the solution of the problems with which Communism deals and for our discussion of the relation between Christianity and Communism?

The first answer to this question is that the existence of this Christian community is the surest bulwark against a totalitarian society. For society to have within it a community that is not the creation of the state, that acknowledges the Lordship of Christ above the state, that magnifies the spiritual freedom of its individual members in relation to all of the powers of the world, that is the bearer of a tradition that is different from any national tradition and from any new ideology that may become the official doctrine of any state, that is universal and encourages fellowship with Christians in all other lands—to have such a community within society is to prevent society from becoming a solid mass that knows only one authority, and it is a protection against the tendency for the state to become God.

I realize that there are dangers in this connection that the Church has not always avoided. When the Church itself becomes a society that seeks to prevent criticism of ecclesiastical authority and then forms a close alliance with a political power, it may be deeply corrupted by such an alliance and also lend a false sanctity to the authority of the state itself. These dangers are not real today in the case of the Protestant churches because of their internal freedom. The Roman Catholic Church in some countries where it is dominant falls into this trap. But Roman Catholicism in countries where it is in a minority can be a strong protection against totalitarianism, and generally it is only fair to say of Roman Catholicism that it preserves a rich religious culture and a system of law which are in the long run resources for humanity against the threat of naked and arbitrary power. The Orthodox Church in Russia is at present engaged in a process of strengthening its position as a church, and in doing this it allows itself to give religious sanction to the policies of the Soviet state. This Church has a background of subservience to political power which is notorious, but its temptations were greater in a nominally Christian culture than they are in a Communist culture. It is still probably true that the Russian Church will be a means of preventing the solidifying of all Russian life around Communist ideology. Its teaching and its liturgy will preserve within the Russian community a non-Communist or non-Marxist tradition. This can be a most important contribution to the Russian future.

So far I have emphasized only an indirect contribution of the Church to society, but there are many other more intentional, more direct forms of influence that it can have in the solution of the problems which cause people to accept Communism. These depend upon the awakening of its members to the reality of the Christian social imperative which has been discussed earlier in this chapter. They depend upon the seriousness with which Christians under the inspiration and guidance of the Church seek to discover the meaning of Christian faith and Christian ethics for the decisions that they must make in the world as citizens, as employers or workers, as members of any one of the professions.

In the United States the Federal Council of Churches[6]

---

[6] The Federal Council of Churches became part of what is now

has exercised leadership in three directions which illustrate what the Church can do in stimulating and guid-
ing public opinion on social issues. Many denominations
have begun to take similar action in a more intensive way
within their own constituencies.

There is, first, the very influential leadership of the
Federal Council through the Commission on a Just and
Durable Peace which helped to form the mind of America in regard to the issue of the peace. It helped to
counteract American isolationism and to make America
ready for an internationalist policy dedicated to the support of the United Nations and to the continuation of cooperation with other nations for reconstruction.[7]

There is, second, the leadership that the Federal Council is now exercising in regard to race relations in America. One of the greatest pronouncements of any church
body in our time was the statement in regard to race by
the Federal Council in its special session in Columbus in
1946, a statement that makes unmistakable the objective
of the American churches that belong to the Federal
Council. The statement was as follows:

> The Federal Council of Churches in America hereby re-
> nounces the pattern of segregation in race relations as
> unnecessary and undesirable and a violation of the gospel
> of love and human brotherhood. Having taken this action,
> the Federal Council requests its constituent communions
> to do likewise. As proof of their sincerity in this renuncia-

---

the National Council of Churches in 1950. The National Council
carries on the same work, and to some extent this work has wider
support than it had under the Federal Council.

[7] This work in regard to international affairs is now being carried on by the National Council's Department on the Church and
International Affairs. This department gives leadership to the
churches especially through its World Order Conferences.

tion they will work for a nonsegregated Church and a non-segregated society.[8]

There is, third, the new department of the Federal Council of "the Church and Economic Life." This department builds on decades of work that has been done on industrial relations but seeks to relate Christian faith to the more complicated problems that have arisen since large sections of American labor have become effectively organized. This department consists of economists, representatives of management, labor leaders, and clergy. It is seeking on a national level and in many local communities to bring together those who represent different interests and points of view so that, under the influence of Christian faith and Christian ethics and in the context of the Church that transcends all conflicting groups, it may be possible to get fresh Christian guidance on the most perplexing economic issues which confront our society. One tangible result of this process so far is that some of the ablest and most articulate leaders of labor who have rarely been seen in church councils are extremely active participants in the work of this department.[9]

---

[8] The National Council of Churches has reaffirmed this position about segregation at its General Assembly in 1952. Most of the national denominations, including those with major strength in the South, have given support to school integration. In many southern communities the ministers have taken a strong stand against the massive resistance against integration which would sacrifice the public schools to the maintenance of racial segregation.

[9] This department, which is no longer "new," has during the past decade supervised quite a massive study of the relation between ethics and economics, and during the process has illustrated in a remarkable way the possibilities in co-operative thinking as between theology and the social sciences as well as between representatives of various segments of the economy.

All of these efforts of a national council of the churches will have no lasting results unless what it does is supported by ministers and laymen in local churches throughout the country. On the local level the going will be harder because local churches are subject to the pressure of the public opinion in the community. But the Christian religion also has its pressure upon those who believe in it and this pressure today is, to a remarkable extent, on the side of real advance toward the overcoming of racial discrimination, toward the realization of more equal justice in economic life, and toward the development of world community.

6

Christianity and the Major Alternatives to Communism

Christianity and Alternative Economic Systems

Christian opposition to Communism should be clearly distinguished from the opposition to Communism by those who oppose it chiefly as an economic system. In the present world struggle between two great centers of power there is much confusion at this point because a large part of the propaganda against Communism and the motives of many powerful groups that influence the anti-Communist policies of governments are controlled by the determination to preserve existing capitalistic institutions. Christianity has no stake in the survival of capitalism.[1]

In Europe and Asia there are many Christians who look both east and west with dread, for though as a rule they see more immediate danger in the extension of the

---

[1] This sentence has been misunderstood. Later in this chapter I mention three elements in capitalism which are permanently desirable. I believe that in any mixed economy some place should be found for these capitalistic ingredients, but the Church should not insist on the kind of mixed economy in which the capitalistic elements are as strong as they are in the United States. Also it should be recognized that capitalism is still a bad symbol in most of the world, as it is generally linked with imperialism.

Communist system backed by Russian power, they see in the thrust of American capitalism a more subtle threat to their national and cultural independence.

There is no Christian economic system. Christianity is older than all existing economic systems. It has no teaching that can be so directly related to the changing conditions of economic life that we can say of any particular economic pattern that it is universally and inevitably Christian. If we were to try to make any system absolute and to give it divine sanction, we would find ourselves in the unfortunate position of all who have tried to freeze history. It is clear that no one of the economic systems that are real alternatives in the world today guarantees all of the values that Christians should seek to conserve. If we keep in mind the importance of the three values, *order* and *justice* and *freedom*, we may readily see how difficult it is for any one system, economic or political, to serve adequately all three values. Constant readjustment will be required, with the emphasis now on one value and now on another, depending on which one has been most neglected. Speaking quite generally, it is the responsibility of Christians to test all economic institutions by their service to those three values and to raise all three of them to higher levels under the compulsion of Christian love.

These values as they become embodied in systems always need to be transformed by love. Take as an illustration "justice." The formal principle of justice is that each person should receive his "due." It is a form of order that prevents arbitrariness. But what is recognized as a person's due changes from generation to generation. It is justice transformed by love that leads some societies to decide that it is the due of every child to have the same opportunities for education as every other child, that where there is a scarcity of milk children of all classes are to be treated as a privileged class. This is now regarded as just in some communities, but it is a new interpretation of justice which is the result of the sensitive understanding of the equal claims of all children because of their special needs and of the recognition that in the case of children equality in rights overshadows all differences. It is justice transformed by love.

What should we say about the relationship between Christianity and capitalism? To begin with, it is important to recognize that there is no such thing as pure capitalism in the form of a fully competitive economy regulated by an entirely free market. This is an abstraction of economic textbooks. America, which is the chief exponent of capitalism, has an economy the freedom of which is interfered with not only by the monopolistic practices of industry but also by labor unions, by government controls, and by a very limited area of government enterprise. We already have a mixed economy in principle, even though it is still dominated by private enterprise. The situation is made all the more confused by the readiness of most groups from the National Association of Manufacturers to the C.I.O. to praise capitalism, while each intends to interfere with the free market for different reasons. It was typical of America that Henry Wallace advocated what he called "progressive capitalism" and that Senator Robert Taft was condemned as "socialistic" by those who stood to the right of him because he believed in public housing.

It is helpful to make a distinction between capitalism as a form of economic organization which involves both private ownership of the means of production and the use of the impersonal forms of regulation that are provided by the free market on the one hand, and capitalism as an "ideology" on the other, that is, as a pattern of ideas which is in large measure the expression of the interests of a class. There has grown up in America, especially in the American business community, an ideology which is as one-sided and as much controlled by class interests as the ideology of Communism. One mark of this ideology is the assumption that the general welfare of a nation is the by-product of the freedom and the profits of the business community. Another mark of this ideology is the habit of emphasizing the dangers and abuses of governmental power and ignoring the dangers and abuses of private economic power. It is also taken for granted that freedom from governmental interference in economic matters is itself a solution of complicated problems which were grievous and unsolved in periods before there was any such governmental interference. Those who see the world through this ideology respond almost automatically to a whole range of issues: labor legislation, tax reduction, price control, government initiative in production, and European socialism. On any one of these issues they might in a particular instance happen to be right, but it is the automatic response that reveals the ideological conditioning. There are many businessmen (for example the members of the Committee on Economic Development) who see far beyond any such ideology and who have a clear grasp of the need for drastic rethinking of the attitudes and policies of American capitalism. Such men are one ground for hope that we may find a middle way which will prevent the recurrence of mass unemployment and still preserve the institutions of political and cultural freedom.

If we can clear away this ideological fog which is the great bane of capitalism as we know it, we may be in a position to recognize that capitalism as a form of economic organization has at least three advantages which should not be lost in any new forms that our economic life may take. The first is that it has always taken seriously the problem of incentive. It offered a far too dogmatic solution of the problem when it gave the impression that the only important incentive is an appeal to unlimited self-interest. But socialistic thinking has not given enough attention to the incentives that are necessary to get efficient production and to call forth new forms of economic activity. Christian teaching should help at this point because its realism about human nature, on the one hand, leads us to expect that it will be necessary to find ways of harnessing the self-interest of men for constructive purposes, and yet it also warns against institutions which enhance self-interest and, because they make a virtue of it, allow it to go undisciplined. It also gives us ground for emphasizing the constructive and unselfish motives which are an essential part of human nature. Contemporary experiments with actual motivations in industry, such as those reported by Elton Mayo,[2] should help to correct dogmatisms of all kinds on the problem of incentive.

Second, capitalism as a method of economic organization has the advantage of encouraging many independent centers of economic initiative. This is a necessary corrective for any scheme which locates all such initiative in the state.

One protection for the pluralistic character of the eco-

---

[2] *The Social Problems of an Industrial Civilization*, Harvard, 1945. One of the conclusions reached in this study is that motives of "self-interest logically elaborated" are actually secondary in industry and that "the desire to stand well with one's fellows, the so-called human instinct of association, easily outweighs the merely individual interest and the logical reasoning upon which so many spurious principles of management are based." (p. 43)

nomic order involving many centers of initiative is the acceptance in principle of various forms of property. There is no form of property that is free from moral dangers, but either total collectivism or unchecked individualism that allows great inequalities in private ownership is clearly evil. There is health in a wide distribution of private property, including private property in agricultural land that is occupied and worked by the owner. Co-operative ownership has great moral advantages in some sectors of the economy. It is as private property becomes a mark of exclusive privilege or confers upon the owner power over others that it needs especially to be kept under rigorous moral criticism. But doctrinaire conceptions of property are as questionable as the doctrinaire formulae for economic systems which accompany them.

A third advantage is that capitalism stands for the value of having at least segments of the economy left to impersonal and automatic forms of regulation instead of attempting to include all economic processes in one vast plan at the center. Christian realism about the sin and finiteness of men provides warning against the attempt to plan everything. Such pretentious planning involves too great concentration of power. It does not allow for the endless variety of experience that is necessary for an understanding of the detailed processes of industry and agriculture. It gives too little place to the dynamic and unpredictable elements in our life.

On the other hand, Christians should be keenly aware of the dangers of anarchy, of allowing people to be at the mercy of impersonal processes when it is possible to control them in the interests of the whole community. Clearly this is an area where there are no *Christian* answers to all questions but where *Christians* have a responsibility to find answers in the light of the values which they seek to serve.

In America, where capitalistic institutions are dominant and where what I have called the capitalistic ideology still, in large measure, controls the middle classes, it is essential for Christians to emphasize the moral limitations of capitalism as they know it.

The Oxford Conference in 1937 enumerated four points of conflict between Christianity and the existing economic institutions. At that time the institutions of capitalism, modified by various social controls, were dominant in Western civilization, though the word "capitalism" was not used in this context because of its ambiguity. These points of conflict were as follows: (1) the tendency of economic institutions to enhance the acquisitiveness of men, (2) the shocking inequalities in economic opportunities and in access to the conditions on which the welfare of all depends, (3) the irresponsible possession of economic power, (4) the difficulty of finding ways of making a living that do not conflict with one's sense of Christian vocation.[3] These still stand as the chief indictments of capitalism in this country, even though there have been improvements because of the increased effectiveness of labor unions (which, of course, also create new problems as well) and because of the use of the political power of the people to correct some of the inequalities and some of the worst abuses of private economic power. It should be noted that those who are most controlled in their outlook by what I have called the capitalistic ideology have fought these advances at every step.

These points of conflict between Christianity and the

---

[3] *The Oxford Conference, Official Report,* pp. 86–92.

dominantly capitalistic order defined by the Oxford Conference include two that are likely to be ignored if we take a purely external and secular view of the issues involved. The "enhancement of acquisitiveness" is one of these. Even if we admit that there is need for economic incentives, it is degrading for the society as a whole to measure success in terms of financial rewards. The place given to the frustration of the sense of Christian vocation suggests the many types of activity in our economy which put a premium upon shrewdness rather than creative work. The Oxford Report calls attention to "salesmanship of the kind which involves deception—the deception which may be no more than insinuation and exaggeration, but which is a serious threat to the integrity of the worker."[4] It would be difficult to say that on either of these points there has been improvement in America since 1937.

We may put beside those four criticisms of capitalism one problem which it has so far shown no capacity to solve on its own terms: the problem of recurring depressions which involve mass unemployment. There is no doubt that, in our time, this failure of capitalism has been the cause of far greater evils than any other of its limitations. Moreover, the people of no nation are likely to tolerate these evils much longer. They will use their political power to change the economic system rather than endure the privations and humiliations of mass unemployment. So both technically and politically the primary test of capitalistic institutions will be their capacity to prevent such unemployment.[5]

---

[4] *Ibid.*, p. 91.

[5] The Amsterdam Assembly of the World Council of Churches in 1948 in the report of its third section also enumerated the criticisms of capitalism. Its list of the defects of capitalism overlapped

It has been natural for Christians who are deeply critical of the existing capitalistic institutions to become Christian Socialists. The Christian Socialist tradition in the modern Church has been an essential corrective for the close alliance between Christianity and capitalism that has been so general in Protestantism. Some Christian Socialists have made the mistake of advocating socialism as though it were an absolute Christian system, and today it is clearer than ever that one should avoid that tendency. Socialism, as a goal, has inspired men to struggle against the human exploitation and the irresponsible waste of resources that have in various degrees characterized capitalism. Christian Socialists were right in learning from Marx and from the socialist movement in general that the industrial workers, because of their special experience of the effects of capitalism and because of the justice represented by their interests and aspirations, have an essential role in bringing into being a better social order. Already, regardless of systems and the labels that have been used to describe them, the effective organization of the workers for economic and political action has been the major dynamic behind the social advances that have been made in all industrial countries.

---

with the one in the Oxford report, but it included also the one emphasized in this paragraph in the following words: "It [capitalism] has also kept the people of capitalist countries subject to a kind of fate which has taken the form of such social catastrophes as mass unemployment." Since Amsterdam the World Council of Churches has abandoned the use of the word "capitalism" to designate a particular economic system. It is too ambiguous a word and there is much confusion when in some circles, mostly in Europe, capitalism is used for a spirit and an ideology which doesn't change, whereas in other circles, especially in the United States, capitalism is used to designate an ever changing combination of economic institutions.

Now that socialism has been partly realized in several nations in both a democratic and a totalitarian form, it is evident that, right as the socialist movement has been in the chief impulse that has driven it, there is no panacea in socialism. It has no magic by which the conflict of interests between various sections of the community can be resolved, as is indicated by strikes against a socialist government. It is tempted to concentrate economic initiative and power in the state. It is in danger of not providing enough incentive to get the necessary work done and to encourage new and varied forms of activity. Unless a community has spiritual and cultural traditions that are on the side of freedom, and unless its people are very vigilant and resourceful, a socialist society may degenerate into a totalitarian society. I hesitate to say this because it is said so often by those whose chief interest is to prevent change of any kind. I should not want to say it without adding immediately that the deliberate choice of a people with democratic experience to socialize their economic institutions is far less likely to prove to be a "road to serfdom" than the drifting of a capitalistic society from crisis to crisis until out of sheer despair its people follow any movement that promises them security even at the expense of freedom.

It might well be deduced from all that I have said about economic systems that Christians will serve society best, not by advocating any system as such or by condemning any system as such, but by helping the community to be sensitive to the human consequences of all systems and by calling the attention of each society to the special dangers that accompany the system dominant within it. In a capitalistic society Christians should seek to provide an antidote for the particular ideologies or blind spots which that society develops, and they should ceaselessly stress the importance of social responsibility and the claims of justice, justice always under the pull of equality. In a socialist society, and in a Communist society where there is freedom to do so, they should help to preserve a realistic view of the actual human situation; they should seek to maintain a measure of pluralism in society, resisting the tendency to subordinate all of the varied interests and energies of the community to an omnicompetent state.

Christianity and Democracy

It may throw more light on the relation between Christianity and Communism to discuss briefly the relation between Christianity and political democracy, which in the conflict with Communism has a much clearer case and far greater moral prestige than capitalism. The issue is confused by the fact that democracy has become a favorite word in the Communist vocabulary. There are obviously at least two quite different meanings of democracy which are behind this confusion.

Democracy as it is used favorably in Communist propaganda refers to the organization of society in behalf of the workers and peasants; it refers to the release, by Communist action, of popular forces which have been suppressed by some previous regime. It is, ideally at least, government *for the people*. It is only to be regarded as government *by the people* if one can accept the claims made by the small Communist minority to represent masses of the people, claims which are highly doubtful in most cases. Even if they have some justification, as may be true of the Soviet Union, there have been years of suppression which have made it impossible for the people to know the full truth about their government or about possible alternatives. There is another limitation surrounding the Communist conception of democracy: "the people" are ultimately limited to those who favor the Communist regime. All opponents soon come to be known as the "antidemocratic" forces, as enemies of the people, and so they do not count.

So, this Communist democracy is in fact the dictatorship of the Communist party on behalf of the people who do count over the people who have no rights because in their opposition to the regime they have become moral offenders. This is not all conscious fraud. It is the natural consequence of the fact that the nations which have become Communist have had no experience of the constitutional liberties that are essential to democracy in its Western sense. It is a natural consequence of the hunger and privation that lead people to put bread and security above all interest in political or cultural liberty and of the deep social conflicts which preclude political tolerance. It gains great moral support from what is believed to be the situation in the United States and in other Western democracies where the poverty and the racial injustice that exist are played up as though they were the substance of Western democratic societies and the political and other constitutional rights are assumed to be purely "formal." There is just enough truth in this caricature of Western democracy to make it seem plausible to people who have had no experience whatever of the ways in which the "formal" institutions of Western democracy can be used to correct the real injustice in its life.[6]

It is Western democracy with which we shall be concerned as an alternative to Communism. It involves two

---

[6] There is a very helpful exposition of the Communist conception of democracy in E. H. Carr, *The Soviet Impact on the Western World* (New York: The Macmillan Co., 1947), chap. 1.

elements which are both indispensable. One of them is government *by the people* with the provision of channels for their political expression. There are here all degrees of direct and indirect democracy and most of this is government by the people through their elected representatives, but there is always the check upon the representatives provided by the power of the people to displace them. The other element in Western democracy is freedom of expression and organization for minorities in an atmosphere of general spiritual and cultural freedom. Freedom is protected by law and by constitutional principles which are essential to the structure of the society and are accepted by the people as a whole. Unless it is possible for minorities to speak and to organize, the minority of today is prevented from becoming the effective political majority of tomorrow, and so the government which begins with majority support would be likely to continue to govern by repression after that support fades. Unless it is possible for minorities to speak and to organize there is no chance to have the continuous criticism of those who exercise power, which is essential in order to limit the abuses which always go with power.

These two elements are essential to the Western form of democracy, but we may add that there are two other elements which have been developed in the experience of the past two or three generations. One is universal suffrage. It is clear that if there is any group that is denied the suffrage, that group is sure to be neglected or exploited. It has no chance to make its interests felt by those who govern and so can be neglected with impunity by politicians. The other new element is the control by the community through government of the powerful economic institutions upon which the welfare of the people depends. The United States has been slow in recognizing the need of this, but since 1932 there has been a gradual revolution in the American system which has done much to correct the plutocratic corruptions of our democracy.

I have gone into this analysis of democracy in its Communist and Western forms in order to make clear what is meant by democracy before raising the question of the relation of Christianity to it. I believe that Christianity does have a stake in the preservation of this Western form of democracy, but before we deal with that, it is necessary to consider two difficulties in suggesting any special relation between Christianity and democracy.

The first is historical. It is obvious that in the past the great Christian churches have not favored democracy. Only the more radical sects that have represented essential corrections of the main Christian traditions were democratic in spirit. Broadly speaking, the main traditions, both Catholic and Protestant, have found constitutional aristocracies more congenial than government by the people as a whole. Even in our own history there was deep distrust of democracy on the part of the older and more established churches which looked with distrust upon the "rabble" that followed Jefferson and Jackson. A republican constitutionalism that was intended to be aristocratic and to favor the rights of property was what the American system meant to many of the founding fathers and to the more respectable and learned of the clergy.[7] Catholicism has always been more at home in the past with conservative and aristocratic regimes than with popular government. There are opposing trends in Catholi-

---

[7] Henry Adams, *The Formative Years*, edited by Herbert Agar (Boston: Houghton Mifflin Co., 1947), Vol. I, pp. 41, 42.

cism and it shows remarkable adaptability to various political systems.[8]

It is important to remember that the Catholic and the Protestant traditions are together, in large measure, responsible for the development of law and of constitutionalism which are an essential part of Western democracy. The logic of Christianity has always been against political absolutism. God, for Christian faith, is above every political power, and the revelation of God's law in the Scriptures has provided a check upon tyrants. If this logic has sometimes been obscured in the past, we now live in a historical situation which leaves no excuse for such distortions. I refer the reader to the discussion in Chapter 5 of the factors that have obscured the Christian social imperative in the past for an explanation of the change that has come in Christian attitudes that are related to the problem of political democracy.

Here it may be enough to state again that the alternatives that confront Christians have changed. The old and "legitimate" authoritarian political regimes that succeeded in convincing themselves and others that they had Christian sanction are in the discard. Nor is the old constitutional aristocracy a real alternative in many countries —an aristocracy, like that in the England of Burke and Wesley, of Johnson and George III, which limited political participation to a small part of the population and

---

[8] The ecclesiastical authoritarianism of modern Catholicism has not made the indirect contribution that the polity of many Protestant churches has to political democracy, and it is difficult for a non-Catholic to see how its indirect influence in the future can be anything else than an aid to political authoritarianism. It is only fair to add that this indirect influence is in some situations counteracted by direct teaching in support of political democracy, especially in the United States.

which permitted very wide areas of shocking social injustice, and yet which was governed by traditions that were intolerant of political absolutism and that provided a great deal of cultural freedom and opportunities for criticism of government. It was undoubtedly social blindness that made many Christians regard such a constitutional aristocracy as a good alternative to democracy; but, at least it was not as clearly evil as the totalitarian state and *there was always something that could be done by organizing to combat particular wrongs.* Today the possibility of concentrating power in government, power that leaves no space for cultural freedom, is far greater. Today in all industrialized countries and in the long run everywhere the people are either going to control a responsible government or they are going to be used in the formation of a tyranny with a mass base and with all of the new forms of power that science has made available to the modern tyrant.

The other difficulty with which we must deal grows out of the fact that a society that is perfectly organized as a democracy, with honest elections and with full freedom for minorities to express themselves, may deliberately choose to be a society that encourages secular or pagan ways of life. It may vote to follow policies based upon a low and hedonistic standard of values or that are isolationist and irresponsible in relation to the needs of other communities. There is no reason to suppose that a democratic society need be in any sense a Christian society. It may use all of the processes of democracy for unchristian or anti-Christian ends. What the people choose to do depends upon the kind of influences which have formed their minds and their consciences.

With these explanations and qualifications I shall now maintain the position already stated, that Christianity has

a stake in the survival of the essential elements in the
Western form of democracy which have been outlined.
This, of course, does not mean that the institutional ex-
pressions of democracy that prevail in America or any
other nation need remain as they are. What has been
said in the first part of this chapter about economic systems should make it clear that capitalism is not necessary as an ally of democracy, that any known economic
system can become a hindrance to it. The essential elements are government by the people and political freedom for minorities in a context of spiritual and cultural
freedom. Of these two elements the second, at this juncture, needs greater emphasis than the first because of the
danger that what appears to be government by the people
may lead to a totalitarian society with a mass base. If
there is one single characteristic of Western democracy
that is more important than any other, it is what we may
call "openness," openness to criticism from all quarters,
openness to truth as transcending power and majority
opinion, openness to God's judgment and to God's spirit
as it comes to the lonely prophet and to the community
of Christians.

The first reason for the Christian stake in Western
democracy is related to the contrast between government
by the people and dictatorships or aristocratic forms of
government. All that has been said about the Christian
social imperative points to the need of having every
group of persons so represented in government that their
needs are not neglected and that as persons they may
have the dignity of sharing responsibility in the decisions
of their community. Christianity knows no second-class
persons, and it is a corollary of this that there should be
no second-class citizens in the commonwealth.

The second reason for the Christian stake in democracy

is that the Christian understanding of human nature warns against any form of uncriticized power, of power that cannot finally be checked by those whose lives are most affected by it. This is a warning that is directed against the old "legitimate" powers that claimed to have a special divine sanction, the rulers or the superior classes who believed themselves to be commissioned by God to rule over the ignorant masses. Godly princes and godly oligarchies have been extremely rare; they never were as godly as they supposed themselves to be and their successors have usually been less so. This was never better said than by Lincoln in his Peoria speech: "No man is good enough to rule another without that other's consent."

This warning is directed quite as much to the new dictators and oligarchs of the left. (It is obviously true of those of the right.) They are not good enough to rule others without their continuing consent and participation; and no matter how noble their ultimate goal may be, that does not confer upon them such goodness. The abuse of power easily becomes the more inhuman and destructive in the new dictatorships than in the old because the background of law and tradition is not there to restrain. One of the most misplaced words in the contemporary discussion of totalitarian dictatorships is to call them "medieval." The Middle Ages were a period of much cruelty, but they were a time when rulers at least had some sense of a law above their own wills and they had some fear of hell. Modern dictators know no such law above them and fear no hell except one of their own making.

The contemporary Christian should be in a better position than his fathers to see how this warning against the way power corrupts those who hold it is to be applied in all directions. There are two illusions that have been natural in various periods, but we have had enough experience to see through them both, not because we are better or wiser than our fathers but because so much has happened to discredit them. There is the illusion of the man in a privileged position who distrusts the "people" but does not see why his own class should be distrusted. There is the man—perhaps an idealistic son of the first who has rebelled against much that his father stood for or he may be one from the "people"—who believes that the "common man" is always right and that any majority of common men can be trusted to use power in the interest of all. He may combine that faith with the conviction that a particular movement of common men has the one true program that will solve most social problems. The American Constitution with its limitation of powers and its checks and balances has the strength that it was based on the recognition of these dangers, though its authors feared the people more than the rule of the wise and the good who usually had property to protect. It can, however, be made to work in both directions and it does stand as a safeguard against totalitarian power.

Reinhold Niebuhr has summarized the Christian case for democracy in an epigram that is unforgettable. He says: "Man's capacity for justice makes democracy possible; but man's inclination to injustice makes democracy necessary."[9] One should be clear that Dr. Niebuhr is referring to the same man in both cases. If we do not believe in the essential dignity and promise of all classes of people, we will not believe in democracy but instead will seek to devise institutions which will enable some people to rule others in order to prevent anarchy. If we do not

---

[9] Reinhold Niebuhr, *The Children of Light and the Children of Darkness* (New York: Charles Scribner's Sons, 1944), p. xi.

believe in the existence of the temptations which go with power, we may be quite willing to acquiesce in any government that is *for the people* even though those in power do not give the people freedom to criticize them or to displace them. The Christian view of man forms the basis of the Christian support of the two essential elements in Western democracy: government by the people and political freedom for minorities in a context of spiritual and cultural freedom.

7

Communism as a Problem in International Relations

CHRISTIAN STRATEGY in relation to Communism must necessarily vary markedly from situation to situation. It will be one thing in Russia or China where Communism has become indigenous and where no reversal may be possible, and where a better future probably depends upon the developments within a Communist society. It will be quite another thing in countries where Communism has clearly been imposed by force from outside and where the winning of freedom from this imposed tyranny is still a hope. It will be different again in countries where there is a strong Communist movement and where there is considerable vulnerability to the appeal of Communism, but where a chance remains to find an alternative. The day-by-day problems of dealing with Communism and Communists in each of those situations call for rare insight and patience and courage, and those who live outside the situation can seldom judge fairly what the real alternatives are for people who live in Russia or China, in East Germany or Hungary, in Kerala or Indonesia, to mention a few examples of situations in which decisions are often difficult.[1] Those who live outside all situations of special Communist pressure may have a certain objectivity and they may help to correct some illusions about Communism, but they are not likely to be able to say exactly what should be done where the pressures are strong. In this chapter I shall deal only with the issues which Christians face in the United States, which is constantly dealing with Communism as a matter of foreign policy.

A few years ago Americans were often victims of hysteria about Communism as an internal threat. In so far as expert attention has been given by government to real cases of espionage or to subversive efforts to influence policy, it has been right. But the nation was chiefly concerned for a short period with the most inexpert hunting of people who at some time within twenty years had had connections with the Communist party or with organizations which served as Communist fronts or who had favored ideas or policies which coincided with Communist ideas or policies. The colossal error during that period was the failure to distinguish between what a person may have done or said or joined in the 1930's from what he may have done or said or joined in the 1950's. To harass anyone in the 1950's for experimenting with what were often disguised Communist fronts in the 1930's, when Fascism, not Communism, was the international danger and when the American economic system seemed to be on the rocks, was as unjust as it was stupid. The character of an organization often changed

---

[1] Dr. Charles C. West in his book *Communism and the Theologians* (Philadelphia: The Westminster Press, 1958) has more wise things to say about the encounter of Christians with Communists as persons under conditions of Communist pressure than anyone else I know. See especially pages 359-387.

in a few years but the names of persons connected with it remained in the Congressional files, even though they had withdrawn from the organization after seeking to counteract Communist influence. Quoting out of context and insinuating that any ideas which were left of center, even when held by the most committed believers in democracy, were signs of Communist sympathies—these were favorite devices.

This widespread panic about the threat of Communism nearly undermined the very liberties which make our society worth defending against Communism. The period of hysteria ended quite suddenly, and this type of persecution of people for their ideas and connections by agencies of government is almost a thing of the past. I mention this as an example of how not to deal with Communism. Among other things it actually weakened the cause of democracy in its competition with Communism.[2]

---

[2] There has been a recent revival of a strong rightist tendency associated with such movements as the John Birch Society and the Christian Anti-Communist Crusade. These movements show a basic lack of understanding of why Communism has gained so much strength in the world. They cannot distinguish between needed social and economic alternatives to Communism and steps toward Communism. They would combine religious hostility against Communism with the political conflict between nations and thus engender the fanaticism of a "holy war." These movements do not have the kind of base within the government that McCarthy had with his capacity to intimidate the Senate and the State Department. They can never win the national support of either major party because they are so conservative on domestic economic issues, but they are a source of much harrassment and they help to create the intransigent attitudes toward cold war issues, especially the tendency to find in Communist nations the embodiments of absolute evil, which bedevil public opinion to a dangerous degree. One curious aspect of these movements is the virulence of their attacks on the Protestant clergy and on the National Council of Churches. Those who want a careful study of the relationship between the Protestant churches and Communism will find it in Ralph Lord Roy's *Communism and the Churches* (New York: Harcourt, Brace, & Co., 1960).

American Christians are related to Communism chiefly through the policies of their nation in regard to Communism as an international force. We are still involved in the cold war with Russia and China. The United States, as the nation that alone can match the military and economic power of the Soviet Union, has a responsibility which it did not choose but which has been thrust upon it. In many ways I envy the citizens of countries that have as much freedom as the United States but that do not have great power and need not face directly all of the decisions which American citizens cannot escape. They can afford to be irresponsible about some issues, and sometimes they can be wiser and more objective on the issue of Communism. It is always a good corrective for Americans to discover that even Canadians see many issues of the cold war in a different light. In keeping up its resolution to play its part as the leader of the non-Communist coalition, the United States is inclined to subject itself to its own propaganda and to become imprisoned in an ideological position almost as rigid as that of the Communists. There are in this respect signs of change in the air, but the fear of being taken in by the wiles and tactics of the Communists makes it difficult to develop a different position in which there is general confidence. In what follows I shall discuss some of the presuppositions which should control the thought of American Christians about national policy.

There is no reason to criticize the two major objectives of policy: the prevention of the extension of Communist power and the prevention of a third world war. These two objectives, which have been the declared aims of policy for more than a decade, should receive strong support from American Christians. The problems emerge when we consider the relationship between these two objectives and when we consider concrete policies for the achievement of either of them.

It has not been necessary until recently to raise the question as to the prior claims of either of those objectives. It could be assumed that, for the most part, both of them could be served by the same policies. As long as it could be assumed that the only possible occasion of war was Communist aggression, it could also be assumed that policies which would provide an adequate deterrent of such aggression would also prevent war. But the development of the nuclear arms race, especially the competition of the United States with the Soviet Union in the production of long-range missiles, has created a danger that war may come either from a technical accident or from a misunderstanding of one another's intentions. The danger that a limited war, against the purposes and plans of both sides, might become a full-scale nuclear war is probably the greatest danger that we face. Now that the deterrent may actually provoke rather than deter war, it is no longer sufficient to assume that the same policies designed to deter the Communist nations from military action will also prevent the war which humanity fears. This means that time, attention, ingenuity, dedicated efforts, need to be concentrated on the specific task of preventing war, of seeking to reduce tensions, of scaling down armaments, of creating areas of disengagement. It is not that we can now say that the prevention even of limited war has such priority that we will run no risks to prevent Communist aggression, but rather that we recognize more clearly that the prevention of war calls for measures of its own and that it is absurd to be so obsessed by the danger of Communism that we are not guided by the fact that an all-out nuclear war would probably destroy the possibilities of a humane and free society for a far longer period than Communism, which as a political system would change or pass away. All-out nuclear war would not only destroy most centers of population and of civilization, it would lead to much genetic distortion among future generations.

Terrible as the nuclear weapons are and unthinkably destructive as a nuclear war would be, the United States as the main nuclear power in the non-Communist world cannot unilaterally renounce the possession of nuclear power as a deterrent. While complacency about the deterrent is no longer possible, we cannot abandon it. We need to supplement it with other policies, and we need to negotiate with persistence and ingenuity within a structure of mutual deterrence to limit the mad missile race, and, if possible, to end it. We need to press for the permanent end of nuclear tests, taking some risks here unilaterally if necessary. If the main drive of our policy in these matters were to be unilateral renunciation of relevant nuclear power, we would probably have less chance of arriving at a stable multilateral arrangement. I am prepared to be convinced that as I say these things there is in my own mind some confusion between what is politically possible for the United States to do and what might be the consequences of a morally adventurous unilateral action. It is quite possible that the latter would have such a powerful effect on the world's political climate that it would not in fact invite aggression. Yet those who are responsible for government do not and probably cannot count on this good possibility, and so, politically, such a policy is well nigh impossible. In this paragraph I have tried to indicate that decisions about policy are agonizingly difficult and that while we should not be obsessed by it, the policy of retaining strong nuclear defense is still a part of our American responsibility. But this policy needs to be accompanied by both attitudes and policies which counteract some of its effects and run in quite a different direction.

1. First, the role of military power needs to be recognized as secondary in the present competition between ideologies and systems. Psychologically it is very difficult to believe at one and the same time that military power is necessary and that it is secondary. It requires such a great national effort to keep up a military force relatively strong enough to act as a deterrent that it is natural to overemphasize its role.

The Russian leaders themselves put great emphasis on their belief that their power resides chiefly in the superiority of their system, and that they want to compete with us in social and economic achievements rather than in military power. Khrushchev keeps returning to this theme. Before his visit to the United States he wrote: *"Peaceful co-existence can and should develop into peaceful competition for the purpose of satisfying man's needs in the best possible way"* [italics his]. He went on to say: "We say to the leaders of the capitalist states: Let us try out in practice whose system is better, let us compete without war. This is much better than competing in who will produce more arms and who will smash whom."[3] He is, of course, confident that capitalism will be "inevitably superseded by Communism—the more progressive and more equitable social system."[4]

These statements of Khrushchev make too much sense, given their assumptions, to be dismissed as mere propaganda. He and many of his colleagues are doubtless sincere in their belief in the inherent weakness of capitalism

---

[3] *Foreign Affairs*, October, 1959, p. 4.
[4] *Ibid.*, p. 6.

and in the inevitable triumph of Communism. This belief is buttressed by two factors in the contemporary situation. One is their own great sense of accomplishment in Russia. The other is the obvious pull that Russian achievements have for the new countries which desperately need to have a social, technological, and industrial revolution and to have it soon. Khrushchev also has quite mistaken views concerning the strength and viability of the semi-capitalist and semi-socialist societies of the West. He sees them through the lens of out-of-date Communist theory, though it should not be forgotten that as recently as the 1930's this theory had some plausibility even in the United States. But however mistaken Khrushchev may be, the fact that it is not unnatural for him to have this confidence in the victory of Communism without war makes it reasonable to assume that he means what he says. Even though he has sometimes tried to discount the extent to which a nuclear war would destroy Communism, he knows that it would destroy most of the Communist achievements. It would be folly for him to gamble with all the gains of Communism when he believes that Russia is well placed for a long competitive struggle.[5]

Quite apart from what Khrushchev says and what he may well believe, is it not obvious that Communist power is not primarily military power? It can leap over

---

[5] There has been some backing and filling in official Communist statements about the degree to which nuclear war would destroy a Communist as well as a capitalistic civilization. Khrushchev's addresses in the United States, especially his address before the United Nations on September 18, 1959, went far in underscoring the threat of war to all humanity. His controversy with the Chinese Communists, which became especially bitter in connection with the Party Congress in 1961, underlines this position.

the best military defenses and render useless the best-drawn security pacts. It is in part the power of an idea but also it is the power to exploit resentments, to take advantage of political weakness and disorder. The chief advantage of Communism is its capacity to convince resolute and self-disciplined minorities in various countries that Communism has the only solution of their problems.

It is now a commonplace to say that the future of Asia and perhaps the balance of power in the world as between Communism and alternative systems depends on the capacity of India to find an alternative to the Chinese method of achieving social change. The Chinese are sure to get much quicker results in industrialization. But can India raise her standard of living fast enough so that her people may hope that she can have a social and economic revolution without sacrificing political democracy and spiritual freedom? This example suggests vividly the limitations of military power in this whole struggle. If India were to fail, it would not be because of military pressure or military invasion; it would be because of the stubbornness of her internal problems and because of Communist effectiveness in organizing a country for rapid social and economic change. Much would depend upon the impression that Chinese institutions make on the outside world during the next decade. And this impression will not depend upon what Americans think of those institutions. Whether or not India is politically and diplomatically neutral, "non-aligned," is unimportant compared with her success in developing institutions which are adequate for her own economic needs and favorable to political and spiritual freedom.

There are important interactions, however, between Communist military power and other forms of Communist power. If there were no balancing military power in the non-Communist world, the presence of a military threat would greatly reinforce propaganda and revolutionary or conspiratorial tactics. People who are on the fence are likely to choose to be on the side of those who have the heavier battalions. But no amount of military power in our control can of itself solve any of the economic and social problems which make nations vulnerable to the appeal of Communism.

In discussing the limits of military power I have emphasized chiefly the new countries which are technologically underdeveloped. Europe is a different matter. Communist advance there at this stage would almost certainly depend upon military attack. A limited war in Europe might be the occasion of such an attack, and such a limited war is not impossible so long as there are such smoldering conflicts as the conflict over Berlin. But surely if the Communists have designs on Europe, they do not want to destroy it first. They may hope that in time the collapse of capitalism will give them a chance to reorganize Europe. Russia has difficulty controlling nations that are close to her borders and in which the democratic tradition is comparatively weak. Why should Russia seek to add to her problems responsibility for the control of the internally healthy countries of western Europe? So long as Russia was herself in the grip of the Stalinist terror, she might have thought in terms of imposing Communism on European nations by a policy of unlimited ruthlessness, but the relaxing of the terror in Russia makes it far more difficult to embark on such a policy.

2. We should accept the fact that Communism is a reality in both Russia and China that will not be over-

come by outside pressure. Actually there is no intention now of trying to destroy Communism in Russia or China, but there is a posture of such hostility on our part that it is not strange that both Russia and China feel threatened by us.

One result of the acceptance of the reality of Communism in Russia and China is that we should be able to recognize that both nations have legitimate interests and reasonable fears as nations, quite apart from the fact that they are Communist nations. The tendency of the American people and even of American policy makers has been to assume that since Communism is evil by definition, Communist nations have neither legitimate interests nor reasonable fears. Not that this is explicitly stated, but it is one of those half-conscious assumptions that condition American thinking. There is no other explanation of the tendency to assume that things that would be intolerable to us if they were done near our borders are justified if done by us and our allies near the borders of Russia or China. This is true of our bases which surround Russia. It is true of our support of the claim of the Chinese Nationalists to the off-shore islands, a few miles from the China coast. It is true of the blindness with which for a decade we have pursued a policy with regard to Germany that envisages a United Germany allied with the West, or latterly an armed West Germany with access to nuclear weapons. Such policies would be unacceptable to any Russian government, and we would not tolerate them if conditions were reversed. The Russian response to our Germany policy is due not to Communist perversity but to the plain lessons of geography and history.

Also there is in the Communist mind at least a residue of fear that at some stage the "capitalistic" countries will attack the citadel of Communism. Walter Lippmann, after his interview with Khrushchev in 1958, came away with the impression that Khrushchev still fears "that if the United States finds that it is going to lose the cold war, it is likely to resort to a hot war." Lippmann goes on to say about this: "That is not what he said, but I came to think that it was what he meant after an interesting passage in which he talked about the American fear and hatred of Communism."[6] If there is much truth in this, certainly one of the major aims of the United States policy should be to try to convince the Russian leaders that this fear is groundless. We also fear to some degree that though Communism does not want to destroy the world but rather to reorganize it, the Communist leaders might at some juncture be tempted to take a military short cut to eliminate American power so that the remainder of the world would be open to Communist penetration. I do not say that this is likely, but the fact that it is a possibility makes it natural to insist on the importance of our power to deter the Communists from such a venture. There is a vicious circle of suspicion and fear. Both sides contribute to it. We can do far more than we are doing to reassure the Russians that we have no intention to use military force at any time to destroy Communism in Russia, or China, and that we really believe in peaceful, competitive co-existence.

China creates more difficult problems today than Russia but I think that what is happening in that country should be regarded as a social earthquake, a vast human convulsion that cannot be understood in terms of our usual moral and political measuring rods. A posture of total hostility does not enable the outside world to deal

[6] *New York Herald Tribune*, November 11, 1958.

with such developments intelligently. Intervention from outside to change the course of events is also futile. Indeed is it not probable that this is an experiment that will have to run its course, and that improvements have to be looked for on the other side of the establishment of the new order rather than in any counterrevolutionary effort to restore an old order?

In such a situation moralistic ostracism is the worst of all policies. This only leads to ignorance in the outside world of what is happening in China and to equal ignorance in China of attitudes and events in other countries. Preparations for relationships between China and other nations should be a minimum objective of policy. Such relationships are necessary for the sake of long-term changes in attitudes, for the hostility is very deep on both sides, but they are also necessary if negotiations in regard to the control of nuclear tests or in regard to other phases of disarmament are to be fruitful. The defense of the people on Taiwan from domination by the Communists is a responsibility which the United States has assumed and which it should share as far as possible with other nations. But this is different from the continuation of our meddling in the Chinese civil war by pretending that the government on Taiwan is the government of China.

It would be a mistake to expect quick results from any change of policy in regard to China. The misunderstanding and the hostility are too deep for that. We can expect many rebuffs, and one favorite exercise for some time to come among statesmen and diplomats is likely to be speculation as to why China does some of the things that she does, as for example the probing on the borders of India. There may be some wisdom in reflecting on how much worse our relations with Russia might be today if a start had not been made in relationships between the two countries nearly thirty years ago. The urgency of negotiations about disarmament, which cannot long omit China, is a new factor that may make all the difference as between those who defend the established policy and those who call for a change.

3. A third quite obvious aspect of the part of American Christian citizens in promoting the cause of political and spiritual freedom against Communism in many parts of the world is attention to the quality of our own national life. Such obvious matters as the achievement of greater interracial justice and constructive dealing with the problem of juvenile delinquency are in the minds of everyone who reflects at all upon the strength of the institutions of freedom in the conflict of systems. We need to emphasize also such less tangible problems of cultural health as the values which are stressed by the mass media and the extent of real spiritual freedom for persons in relation to the giant economic organizations which control their lives. It is often said that to the outsider Soviet society and American society are two societies dominated by the same materialistic values, even though our practical materialism goes against the religious professions which still prevail among us whereas the Soviet practical materialism is supported by the official philosophy. I think that more important even than this issue of practical materialism is the issue of real freedom of choice, of real freedom to express convictions on controversial questions which our people have. The state is not the enemy of their freedom as in Communist countries; rather it is the private economic organization and the pressure of local public opinion. To be sure, among us there is more diversity among private organizations,

and there are differences in the climate of opinion in various localities and in various social strata. But we need to watch especially the subtle influences which restrict freedom.

The main issue between the open societies and Communist societies is not over the pattern of the economic system. As I have said in an earlier chapter, Christians as such are not defenders of "capitalism" and it is quite possible that, given several decades, capitalism and Communism will be mixed systems which resemble each other more than they differ. But in the short run there is danger that emphasis in the United States on individualism in economic life may be carried so far in relation to needed public services, and that our society will lag so far behind the Soviet society in matters of public welfare, that the uncommitted nations will be the more easily convinced that Communism as an economic system would be best for them. They might then be drawn into Communism as a total system of life. Professor Kenneth Galbraith has done a great service in calling attention to the extent to which great prosperity in this country in terms of private wealth is combined with public poverty in those aspects of the economy in which government must take major initiative. We are poor in our educational system in relation to the needs of our growing population. We lag in housing for low-income groups. We allow millions to suffer because of lack of available medical care who, if they lived under a Communist or Socialist system, would receive the needed care. We are only beginning to deal with the economic problems of our retired people, who represent a rapidly increasing proportion of the population. Even our public transportation system is breaking down, with no serious effort on the part of the government to develop an efficient and well co-ordinated transportation system.[7] To plunge almost blindly ahead with a dogmatic faith in the self-sufficiency of free enterprise as our major guide may not create a society in the United States which will be attractive to other nations where a higher value is placed on the social welfare made possible by public services—nor can such a free system maintain itself in this country. Neither a hectic imitation of Russia's emphasis upon science and technology nor a desperate effort to preserve our present forms of free enterprise are likely to enable us to compete successfully with Communism. Rather we should keep our minds open to what measures now will best serve the substance of spiritual and cultural freedom and the social welfare of the whole society. No combination of measures from a previous decade will be sufficient.

An essential part of our national character which will have great bearing on the conflict of systems is our attitude toward other nations, especially the new nations which are seeking to find their way, to develop political institutions, and to overcome their inherited poverty. We need to be open to their various experiments in which they engage without measuring all that they do by narrow American political and economic criteria. We should be generous, not in the sense that we give away things for which we expect gratitude, but in the sense that we really take seriously our solidarity with them, that we regard it as intolerable for us as well as for them that there be such vast differences of wealth between their countries and ours.

---

[7] John Kenneth Galbraith, *The Affluent Society* (Boston: Houghton Mifflin Co., 1958). See especially chap. XVIII, "The Theory of Social Balance."

Herbert Butterfield has written that "the greatest menace to our civilization is the conflict between giant organized systems of self-righteousness." "Each system," he says, "only too delighted to find that the other is wicked —each only too glad that the sins give it the pretext for still deeper hatred and animosity."[8] I may betray my own participation in one of these systems by saying that the other system is better organized than ours, that it is encased in a much more complete suit of ideological armor. But it is important to realize that our system of self-righteousness is a reality and that there has long been a vicious circle between ours and theirs. Within the Church there is always a major responsibility to keep the Christian faith from being the means of hardening any system of self-righteousness, to help its members to see both systems under the righteousness of God and to realize how far both are from his righteousness, to see the opponents—in this case the Communists—as people who are not mere creatures of ideology, as people who are influenced in their minds and in their lives by historical experience. Can both systems of self-righteousness be cracked a little at the same time? There is more hope of this as I write than there has been at any time since the beginning of the cold war. Christians are called to pray and to work that this may happen.

---

[8] Herbert Butterfield, *Christianity, Diplomacy, and War* (Nashville, Tenn.: Abingdon Press, 1954), p. 43. Professor Butterfield's book *International Conflict in the Twentieth Century—a Christian View*, published by Harper in 1960, is a radical challenge to thinking conditioned by the cold war, and it may prefigure what will be, within another decade, the common assumptions of sane men.

8

Some Moral and Religious Objections to Co-existence

THERE ARE many people who find the prospect of co-existence with Communist nations to be morally repellent and reject it. The association with Communist leaders who have been involved in ruthless acts of oppression and the acceptance of Communism as a reality that has come to stay, rather than as an absolutely evil power which we vow to destroy, are condemned as a betrayal of all who have been victims of Communism. In the United States the visits of such Communist leaders as Deputy Premier Anastas I. Mikoyan and Premier Nikita Khrushchev have been occasions for outpourings of indignation by some groups against their reception as human beings with whom it is morally appropriate to deal. Their reception seems to put a stamp of at least partial approval on their past and present exercise of power. Exiles from Russia and, even more, from Baltic countries which have been cruelly destroyed as nations and absorbed into Russia, and from the European satellites, especially Hungary, have provided much of the stimulus for this moral criticism of a policy of co-existence. Many Roman Catholic leaders have taken the same position and they tend to emphasize the avowed godlessness of Communism and its persecution of religion. What should we say about this view of co-existence?

I think that if there were no signs of improvement in Russia and if we were dealing there with the full Stalinist reality, there would be much to say for this view. I confess I had similar feelings when I saw the pictures of Andrei Vishinsky with his smiles when he was the Soviet representative at the United Nations. He had been chief prosecutor in the Stalinist purge trials in the 1930's. Whatever his motives and rationalizations as a Communist, he did symbolize those terrible deeds of blood. One cannot but sympathize to some extent with groups of exiles who are controlled chiefly by memory of past wrongs.

The basic reason for rejecting this view is that we must consider the future rather than the past. Any tolerable future that we can now foresee depends upon critical and competitive, but also partly co-operative, co-existence with the Soviet Union. Those who insist on perpetuating the crusade against Russian Communism do not help any of the present victims of Communism, and they may prepare the way for war and themselves come to share moral responsibility for the victims of war. The people of Hungary and of other nations which have been victims can be helped best by a period of relaxation of international tensions, for Russian action in Hungary was controlled in part by fear for her own security, fear that was in terms of her assumptions justified. If there is much truth in what I have said in the discussion in Chapter 3 about the changes that are taking place in Russia, these changes are more likely to go forward if there is less international tension; and it is worth while, for the sake of the very people who are now victims, to try to find a *modus vivendi* with the Soviet Union which will enable these changes within Russia to continue. The future of the people of the satellites can be served best by astute pressures on their part while the Russian methods of control become more moderate. Liberation by force would probably destroy the liberated.

We need to deal with this problem on two other levels —one the level of moral judgments about Communists, and the other the level of discussion emphasized by those who stress the godlessness of Communism.

It is a profound mistake to treat Communists, even powerful ones, as though they were gangsters or criminals. If this were what they are, the problem which they create would be far simpler than it is. As I have emphasized in this book, many men have become dedicated Communists from high motives. In doing so they have acquired serious illusions, some of them moral illusions, that have had fateful consequences. But it is a mistake for us to fail to see that Communism is at its center a gigantic effort at construction, though it is accompanied by ruthlessness that is abhorrent. It is believed to be a short cut to an ideal society and the moral quality of the individual Communist can only fairly be judged in this light.

Also, it is only fair to stress the point that I made in my discussion of the Communist attitude toward violence, comparing it with the attitude of many of us who are non-Communists toward violence in war.[1] The violence that accompanies tumultuous events, wars and revolutions, creates a terrible problem for all of us. The sharing of responsibility for the massive destruction of such cities as Dresden and Hiroshima is not as morally different as we may prefer to think from sharing responsibility for the ruthless acts of Communists when they are engaged

---

[1] See chapter 4, pages 89-96.

in a continuous war against a supposed enemy. In both cases the ultimate goal is believed to be a good one that requires means that are morally abhorrent. It has been easier to limit international war to a particular period of time than it is to limit revolution, and this enables those of us who shared responsibility for the conduct of war to put the ethics of war in brackets and separate them from our normal ethics. Communist persecution of helpless people who are at hand may corrupt them more than we were corrupted by acts of total destruction against millions of people at a distance, people whose suffering we never saw. (If this is true, the reasons for it would make an interesting study.) In any case, our black and white moral judgments are inadequate in assessing the personal character of persons caught within various kinds of violent struggles. Living with people with repellent deeds of violence in their past is not a problem limited to our living with Communists!

But again, let me emphasize that my chief concern is about the future. To insist on keeping old wounds open perpetually for moral reasons would lead to the most morally destructive disasters. There is a kind of moral "statute of limitations" operating in the lives of nations. In part this is the forgetting of past evils as we become concerned with new ones that have different sources; in part it comes from the recognition that a new generation has arisen which had little or no responsibility for the particular evils that once aroused greatest condemnation. Nations which we count very respectable were once involved in atrocities which were vigorously condemned. This is true not only of Germany and Japan which have renounced former regimes; it is also true of a country like Turkey where the same regime is in power that was responsible for the atrocities. To dwell now upon the evils in the past would not help their victims and it would shut the door to constructive developments. This moral "statute of limitations" resembles a historical process of forgiveness even when there is little conscious repentance in the lives of nations. There may appear to be an element of moral indifference in it but there is also wisdom in it, for without it there can be no healing.

Much of the emotion behind the moral rejection of co-existence comes from the fact that Communist nations are officially godless, that in various degrees they have been guilty of religious persecution. Actual persecution is not the problem in Russia, but even there the Church is limited in its public witness and in its education of its youth, and the state does carry on vigorous but not very effective propaganda for atheism. In general there are numerous efforts to hinder religion and to make the profession of religion a handicap to personal advancement. In other Communist countries, especially China and East Germany, the pressure against the churches is much worse. It is natural that in these circumstances many people in the West would desire a religious crusade against these godless nations.[2]

I suggest three criticisms of this attitude.

The first is that churches should take seriously, as I have said before in this book, their own responsibility for the atheism of Communism. It is a great tragedy that

---

[2] It has often been noted that as between Catholicism and Protestantism there is a difference in tendency in regard to relations with Communism. Catholicism tends to emphasize the dogmatic differences between Christianity and Communism and to make much less of the historically conditioned factors in Communism which may qualify the absolute ideological conflict. But American Catholic leaders are often more intransigent on any issue which has a Communist aspect than is the Vatican itself. There is far greater flexibility among Catholics in some other countries, in

when the Marxist movements took shape in the nineteenth century they became anticlerical, antireligious, atheistic. This was in part a reflection of a pseudo-scientific rejection of orthodox Christianity which was characteristic of the period, but the drive behind it was due more to the failure of the great churches in Europe to understand the industrial revolution and to champion the cause of its victims. I have enlarged on this before but at this point in the discussion it is most relevant. A self-righteous religious crusade against Communism that discourages all efforts at *rapprochement* between our government and Communist governments, that encourages a policy of moral ostracism of Russia and China, is a great mistake. It ignores the real roots of Communist atheism. When churches take this line they encourage the worst in themselves; they become vehicles of hatred, with religious passion adding its fury to political conflict.

The second suggestion is that no religious victims are going to be helped by this attitude. The deeds of the past cannot be undone. The future will be less stained with blood if the impasse between the two worlds can be overcome sufficiently to scale down armaments. Political moderation in Communist countries may be accompanied, as in Russia, by cessation of direct persecution. The struggle of Christians against disabilities of various kinds will continue as a spiritual struggle, and it will not

France especially, than here. Also in Poland Catholics have learned to live with a Communist regime and to make the most of a difficult situation. The World Council of Churches has consistently tried to preserve relationships between Christians on both sides of the Iron Curtain in spite of all criticisms of the kind of adjustments which have been made under Communist regimes. I believe that this policy of preserving relationships has proved sound even though in detail it has led to some serious confusions.

be helped by this kind of religio-political crusading by Christians in non-Communist countries against Communism.

The third suggestion is that Christians in all countries should seek opportunities for relationships with people in Communist countries. Ostracism of Communist nations and religious warfare against them will unnecessarily postpone the day in which such relationships become possible. The number of wholehearted, fully convinced Communists in any country is relatively small. The number of people who have grown up under Communism and who are loyal to their country and its regime, and whose mental outlook is limited and distorted by Communist teaching, is very large in Russia, and it may well be large in China. To declare a holy war on a Communist nation as a whole is to alienate these people as well as the convinced Communists. It also makes more difficult the role of churches within Communist countries. Instead, churches in the West should plan for every possible new relationship or restoration of relationships which can be the means of healing conflicts and which may once again make possible Christian witness to those who have long been cut off from the gospel.

Even if Communism is relatively successful as an instrument of social, technological, and industrial revolution, it is a miserable substitute for religion. Its blindness is the source of errors about man and society which will become apparent as the early decades of excitement, the excitement of revolution and the excitement of building the foundations of the new society, pass. Surely as this is God's world there will be new openness to Christian truth where Communism holds power. Churches which have abandoned self-righteous hostility and which are prepared to establish relationships can speak to such openness. But more important than such speaking will be the re-established relationships between individual Christians and persons influenced by Communism when doors once more are open.

9

The Policy of Christians in
Relation to Communism

IN ANALYZING the conflict between Christianity and Communism I have tried to bring out the valid elements in Communism, especially the valid elements in the Communist criticism of the churches and of cultures that have claimed to be Christian.

Those who are attracted by Communism because they know that civilization needs a radical cure, and that Communism alone seems radical enough, have a sound starting point. The tragedy is that they soon become blind to the elements of sheer reaction in Communism when it gains power. Either they must believe that this phase of reactionary oppression is incidental to revolution and will soon pass or they must believe that the victims of this oppression, as enemies of the new order, deserve nothing better. The first belief is as yet supported by no evidence, and the second belief does not take account of the tendency of dictators to be guided by their fears and to turn into enemies all who could conceivably threaten their power—including the more idealistic among their own original adherents.

Those are right in intention who are attracted to Communism because they want to be part of a movement of the "people," believing that only the industrial workers and the peasants and the landless laborers on the land and the hosts of those who have always lived under the blight of race discrimination—only those who know in their bodies and in their daily experience the darkest side of civilization that is hidden from most of the readers of these words—can form the political instrument that will bring real emancipation. The vision and the dynamic born of such experience have usually been lacking in the councils of the Church and even in Christian movements for social action. Again it is tragic that, essential as this vision and dynamic are, they are used by the Communist movement as the means for gaining power to establish a new regime which acquires its own grim dynamic as it destroys its old critics and opponents and ceaselessly intimidates those who might become new critics and opponents of its own abuse of power.

The conflict between Christianity and Communism is closely related to the conflict between democracy and Communism, in so far as democracy stands for the continued openness of society that keeps the power of old and new regimes alike under criticism and provides the means by which injustices can be corrected. The institutions of spiritual and cultural freedom on which this "openness" depends have grown in soil prepared by Christianity. Without them Christians themselves are likely to be driven underground or their religious expression so limited that there can be no public teaching of the faith. Also, without them the rights of expression that Christians regard as essential to the development of persons are consciously and systematically denied.

The American Christian is in a very great moral difficulty. He is tempted to identify this conflict between Communism and essential elements in Western democracy with the conflict between Communism and capitalism, and even with the conflict between Russian and American power in the world. But it is a profound error to make either identification. The democratic socialists of Europe are as much opposed to Communist totalitarianism as he is, and he should avoid altogether the tendency to give religious sanction to capitalism. He must be quite clear that while American power in some situations is a necessary resource to prevent Russian power from closing the door on political freedom, it often seems to other nations to be a threat to their economic freedom.

The American Christian should be especially watchful when hysterical fear of Communism on the part of economic conservatives and the zeal of military branches of his own government seek to prepare the minds of the American people for a military showdown. There is a military side of the resistance to the extension of Communism that must not be overlooked, but it is secondary. It is secondary both because military victory over Russia and her Communist allies would save none of the real values which Communism threatens and because the power of Communism is not primarily military.

The chief function of the military in the resistance to Communism is to make it clear to Russia that it would be too costly for her to force a military showdown if at any time the Kremlin should be tempted to take such a short cut to power. It is essential that American military strength be kept under civilian control, not in a formal sense but in the sense that it should remain one part of an inclusive policy that is administered by men who understand the nature of Communism and who are careful to take no steps that will aggravate the Russian fear of an aggressive intention on the part of America. One of the most perplexing factors with which Americans must deal is the apparent conviction of the Russians, based upon Marxist dogma, that a declining capitalistic state is sure to make war to escape from the inner contradictions of capitalism and to destroy such a citadel of Communism as the Soviet Union. It is probable that while Russia is positively aggressive in her attempt to extend Communism, her military preparations are primarily defensive in purpose. Her real aggressive strength lies in the power of Communism to win its way by propaganda and infiltration.[1]

Military victory over Communism would be so destructive that it would multiply many times the number of desperate people in the world who would snatch at any hope of security against anarchy and hunger at whatever cost to freedom.

The real power of Communism is based upon the fear and privation following the destruction of so much of Europe, upon the desire of peasants on several continents to be rid of feudal forms of oppression, upon the aspirations and resentments of the colored races, and upon the unsolved problems of capitalism, especially the expected catastrophic depression which, according to Com-

---

[1] I realize that any opinions about Russian intentions are debatable, but the analysis of Edward Crankshaw, author of *Russia and the Russians*, in the *New York Times Magazine*, July 4, 1948, makes good sense in view of what we do know. He shows how utterly unwarlike the Russian people are and then he says: "Their rulers, on the other hand, have never hesitated to use force or the threat of force to attain their immediate ends when they considered, sometimes wrongfully (as in the case of Finland in 1939), that a small, sharp effort would be successful. But almost invariably their objectives have been strictly limited and local; they have never started a large scale war, and the Russian tradition is to use force only for the *coup de grace*, when their opponent has been weakened by other means. This Russian tradition fits in to perfection with Communist tactics, which do not include a frontal attack on a strong position."

munist schedule, will undermine the strength of the West. It is these sources of Communist power to which American Christians should direct major attention. They should begin at home and prove that it is possible to prevent mass unemployment without having recourse to tyranny from right or left, that the institutions of freedom are not merely "formal" as Communists allege but that they really are the means by which society can be continuously corrected in the interests of justice.

There is one concluding consideration. The strength of Communism consists also in the fact that it provides a faith for living for millions of people, especially young people, who have never encountered any faith which put so much meaning into life and which so adequately related their social aspirations and ideals to an interpretation of the world. As Alexander Miller says: "To them Communism presents itself as the most coherent philosophy and the greatest single emotional drive that this generation has to deal with."[2] Much has been said in earlier chapters about unsound elements in this faith, but it would be a mistake to underestimate its persuasiveness to those whose own social experience has prepared them to receive it.

There is no other faith which can compare with Communism except Christianity. Christianity, when its full meaning is not hidden by one-sided teaching or distorted by alliances between the Church and privileged groups, is a faith that can meet the need of those who struggle for more equal justice in the social order. It will also prepare them to be radicals in any new order, for it will help them to understand how quickly new institutions and

---

[2] Alexander Miller, *The Christian Significance of Karl Marx* (New York: The Macmillan Co., 1947), p. 2.

new collocations of power may become the source of new forms of injustice. It will also enable them to relate all that they may do for the transforming of society to the depths of their personal lives and to the ultimate purpose of God. The first responsibility of the Christian community is not to save any institutions from Communism, but to present its faith by word and life to the people of all conditions and of all lands, that they may find for themselves the essential truth about life.